# START FROM ZERO

## BUILD YOUR OWN BUSINESS
## EXPERIENCE TRUE FREEDOM

# DANE MAXWELL

Publisher: Jesse Krieger
Get Published: Jesse@JesseKrieger.com

Printed in the USA

Do you have the spark inside to create
something *of your own?*

$$((((( \quad \text{✦} \quad )))))$$

This book will show you how *to follow that spark.*
Even if you are starting from zero.

Meet other people reading this book at
StartFromZero.com/Yes

# CONTENTS

# BEGIN WITH THANKS

## How Can You Ever Say Thank You Enough?

**This book would not exist without many things...**

First, I want to thank the authors of the books I read before me. My brain would be lost without your passion, knowledge and writing. Much of the world projected confusion onto me when I was starting a business out of college. I felt like the odd man out. Many people would try to encourage me to get a job. Tell me to "go work downtown in a suit," but I kept my head inside the books and listened to those voices, not the world.

It worked.

Thank you.

Thank you too my beautiful partner Jacqueline and my beautiful daughter Everly, for helping me open my heart, that's a wild and magical and frightening experience. You two are the brightest lights in my life.

Thank you to my parents who encouraged me when I decided to start my own business at 22. For letting me move into the basement for a year. And then for kicking me out after a year.

Thank you to my sisters for believing I was capable.

And then to all of the healers! I hired many, because my brain haunted me often haha. Healers are often forgotten and give more of themselves without much recognition in return.

The late Dr. Barry Green, for all our time together.

Dr. Douglas J. Tataryn, for standing for me to see my patterns.

Dr. Justine Anderson, for showing me I have a beautiful heart.

Jacqueline Marie, for helping me stand in the light of love no matter the hatred I feel.

Brian Adler, for ending my search, and showing me peace was here now.

Thank you too Andy Drish, for getting my butt into the limelight to share this message. I never believed I was good at teaching until you forced me to believe so.

Rachel Kersten, for holding me to such a high standard it's almost unbearable. Thank you.

To my uncle Robb Spearman who gave me my first customers in business when I could hardly handle starting something.

Daniel Reifenberger, for reading and helping me think through parts of this book and being a great friend.

Ralph Benjamin, for treating me with a deep respect and seeing me as beautiful when I thought the world had turned against me.

Thank you to Sara Stibitz for telling me this book needs work when I submitted the first draft. You were right, thank God I listened.

Thank you to Jesse Krieger for being my publisher and helping me. And telling me I'm one of the most qualified people you know to teach this kind of book.

There are many people I could thank, if I for some reason have missed you, I'm sorry. It's hard to keep track with so many generous people.

Acknowledgment is important. We need more love than we think we do to start something. I got more love than I realized. The truth is while I started a business from nothing, I always had love available.

Let this book be the friend you've been looking for. Let it guide you safely into the world of entrepreneurship.

# SUMMARY

## This Book Summarized in 4 Pages

The book is about you.

In it, you will go on seven learning adventures.

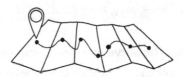

The goal of this book is for you to build the brain of an entrepreneur. One that can build meaningful businesses and income streams from nothing. This book is perfect for either a starting entrepreneur or someone with an existing business looking to scale their product revenues.

I created this book to sit on your nightstand and become a companion on your journey. Let it be your friend along the way.

Here are the seven big learning adventures in this book.

### Adventure 1: Learn The Three Little Rocks
These rocks—the single most important question, the cardinal rule of successful entrepreneurship, and dealing with jealousy—will be your weapons against being poor, lazy, and stupid.

### Adventure 2: Learn What You Don't Need

 Here you'll see entrepreneurs are just as flawed as the rest of us. Often they are more flawed; they just make up for it by hiring great teams. Learn the advantages you can use instead of the barriers you have now.

### Adventure 3: Learn What You Do Need

Here you'll transform what you think of yourself on an identity level and deal with fear. With this transformation in place everything else becomes easier and automatic.

### Adventure 4: Learn The Four Brains

Very few entrepreneurs possess all four of these brains. In fact most entrepreneurs get by with just two or three. But if you combine all four, your bank account will look very, very good.

**Brain One: The Surveyor** – Here you see the world in income streams and survey landscapes. Once you understand this, you'll see income streams everywhere.

**Brain Two: The Tiller** – Here you find and sell ideas by tilling the landscape you surveyed. This is a very profitable skill when done correctly.

**Brain Three: The Planter** – Here you create and plant scalable product seeds from scratch. The planter is thorough and masterful.

**Brain Four: The Gardener** – Here you garden and grow the product revenues. Many activities are a waste of time; only a few are needed to grow revenue.

## Adventure 5: Learn The 7 Skills

 In entrepreneurship there are hundreds of skills you could learn. The following 7 skills will allow you to sell stuff, outsource stuff, learn from screw-ups, and be the owner.

**Skill One** – Using Words That Sell: Here you'll learn the greatest skill of all — selling with the printed word. It'll make you very, very successful.

**Skill Two** – Ownership vs. Expert Thinking: Here you'll learn why being the owner, and not the expert, is where the wealth resides. It's a peculiar skill. It requires healthy self-esteem. And once you understand it, you'll stop trying to be an expert.

**Skill Three** – Being a Newbie. At the root of extreme success is an element of "moving forward" while "not knowing." Experts like to be right. Owners like to not know and figure it out. Here you develop a trust for figuring things out and start appreciating being a newbie instead of frowning upon it.

**Skill Four** – Developing Outcome vs. Process Thinking: Here you'll see that mediocre productivity and struggling businesses don't really focus on outcomes. Businesses that place outcomes first as a priority are very successful.

**Skill Five** – Income Happiness. Not all dollars made are equal. Some dollars can suck your soul, and some are awesome. Here you'll learn how to set up your profit so it is efficient and guard your heart so the environment is pleasurable.

**Skill Six** – Learning from mistakes, losses, and low-integrity moments: What do you do when you know you've screwed up bad? Here you'll see a terrible mistake I made, how I handled it, and what I have learned.

 **Skill Seven** – How to Make the Biggest Leaps. Most people are careless and stingy with their money. Here you'll see how I took quantum leaps when I was 24 years old by knowing where to spend my savings and where not to.

### Adventure 6: Learn The 4 Growth Levels of an Entrepreneur

Once you've begun your entrepreneurial journey, use this as a map for how to stay focused, evolve, and grow. From beginner to pro, this final chart will show you where you are on the map and how to make sure you don't lose focus.

### Adventure 7: Learn 15 Examples Of Starting From Zero in the Halls of Transformation

Here you'll see 15 different students who have transformed who they thought they were and built businesses that provide them with freedom. I have broken down the aspects of each of these businesses, and you can see how they got started.

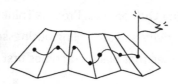

### Bonus Adventures – All Of The Extra Goodies On One Page

Visit StartFromZero.com/Yes for access to every bonus on one page clearly organized, with no email capture required.

### More Resources: What To Do Next...

When you're ready for more, here you'll see more book recommendations and resources to jump-start your journey.

# THE THREE LITTLE ROCKS

You are about to embark on the journey of a lifetime! It will be quite an adventure. Before you go on your voyage, I want to give you three little rocks to put in your pocket. Use these rocks and symbols as reminders or keepsakes.

Keep them in your pocket so they are always with you. Do not forget them.

## Little Rock Number 1
## The Daily Question for Getting Rich
## & Staying That Way Forever

If you'd like to protect your financial future, get rich, become free, and always be financially safe, then this is the most important question you'll ever need to ask. You can ask it at the end of each day before you lay down for bed. You must answer yes to this question, or you are at risk.

That question is: *Did I build any equity today?*

For many of us, when we step back from our day and reflect, we will see that we have not built any equity with our actions. We will see we have exchanged time for money. We will see we have spent our most valuable resource of time, for something that is so readily exchangeable.

Money.

I truly don't get why a human heart would want to trade their most valuable resource so easily without building equity. Money isn't everything. That's why you shouldn't spend your most valuable resource to get it.

Every day that you wake up to work, you must be building equity or building towards having equity.

What is equity? Put simply, equity is ownership in something that can produce cash or be sold without your direct time on a day-to-day basis. Having equity is having an asset that provides for you and your family.

*It is not that hard to build equity.*

Think about this. Most of us have spent 10-plus years learning how to be an employee. If you spent even one year learning how to build equity, you'd know how to do it. It's not hard; it is simply a matter of training.

It's a matter of building a different brain. It's a matter of learnable skills. You can learn these skills. Don't let anyone tell you otherwise.

Think about the difference between building equity each day and not building equity and how that difference would affect your life. The compound effect of building equity every day is the key to security. That's why the rich keep getting richer.

My business friends and I build equity every day. You can join us. This book will show you how to build equity every single day for the rest of your life.

# Little Rock Number 2
# The Cardinal Rule of Successful Entrepreneurship

Before we begin, you must—and I mean, *must*—understand the most critical rule of wildly successful entrepreneurship. Break this rule and screw yourself. Follow this rule and become wildly rich.

I've met entrepreneurs who earn over ten million per year become proud and break this rule, only to get hammered for it.

This rule may seem foreign at first, but this rule eliminates all of my fear around making money. You will understand it by the end of this book. And you'll be richly rewarded for it.

Here is the rule: We do not get to decide what works.
That's.
It.

When you realize that all you have to do is listen, you'll wonder why you didn't do this years ago.

If everything crumbled to the ground, I would not fear because I would simply go out into the world and listen deeply to the pulse of what works and create wealth around that, trusting that something would emerge. Too many force their own ideas on markets or people only to become frustrated, fail, and give up.

Blaming others. Like idiots. Ignoring this rule.

Wealth and freedom as taught in this book are not about guessing what works or coming up with an idea like Facebook or Craigslist. Or Facebook meets Craigslist.

It is about listening.

This sounds simple, but it's rather difficult. As you read the pages of this book, you'll start to understand this rule. And if you ever find yourself trying to be smarter than this rule, or smarter than the people you are serving, swallow your pride, open your heart again, and listen.

I still forget this rule. I think we all do from time to time. If you ever catch me trying to be smarter than you, you have my permission to shout, "S-Y-P."

Swallow.
Your.
Pride.
Then I'll remember to open my heart again and start listening.

## Little Rock Number 3
## Handle the Jealousy Trap With
## Open-Hearted Curiosity

If you are jealous, you are screwed. It's a low-vibration experience that shuts off all creativity.

All.
Creativity.

Have you ever felt jealous of someone else, someone's product, or their business? Being jealous slows you from moving forward, cripples you from seeing cleary, and it shuts off learning as well.

Jealousy locks you into place.

Here's the thing... jealousy (and envy) are emotions we all feel. Even so, I don't see these emotions being addressed in business books, and that's why this little rock is here.

Don't make the same mistake I have made. I have found myself in a state of jealousy for years, and it kept me from moving forward (and this was after all my initial success too)!

I was stuck on a plateau because of fear, and that created jealousy. I was too afraid of my own power, so I sat envious of others who did what I was too scared to do. So many of us cripple our own happiness and potential because of this trap.

You can drop the jealousy (and envy) by asking one simple question. Open your heart and ask yourself this...

> "What can I learn from this person, product, or business that I am jealous of? What qualities do they have that I actually admire?"

Your envy will calm and your curiosity will emerge as you see that there is something there for you to learn. You'll start to feel more free and creative. You'll start to feel whole instead of fragmented, and you'll take your power back—immediately.

This question requires humility, but humility is deep power. Don't give your power away with jealousy, arrogance, and envy like I did.

You can choose Joy by asking this question and taking full responsibility for your own life. Joy is a super power in business.

**Now we are ready to begin.**
Armed with these three little rocks you will have a more enjoyable time on your journey down the road of entrepreneurship. You'll fight with reality less, you'll relax more, and you'll take more responsibility for your success.

Let's turn the page and get started on your adventure.

## I Owe My Life & Self Esteem To Business

Everyone deserves to feel personally significant.

And business was the first place I found a sense of personal significance. Up until that point, I felt like I didn't belong anywhere in the world.

I was treated poorly as the slow, stupid, ugly kid. I was badly bullied, tortured, and even spit on. I did not feel valued by others. My parents were great. The world...not so much. But I was so ashamed I never told anyone what happened. Until now in this book.

And so my heart closed for 22 years...until I found entrepreneurship. Entrepreneurship was the place I could open my scared heart again.

But I'll save you the details on my life story, because that's not what this is about.

This book is about you. Finding and creating epic freedom. I just want you to know business is about so much more than freedom. It's a place to find yourself.

It took me a long time to find a sense of belonging. I spent the first 22 years of my life searching for acceptance and finally found it for myself in entrepreneurship.

I didn't feel ugly here. I didn't feel bullied. I felt significant. I felt valued.

I found a place for my heart to land and for my self-esteem and confidence to grow.

When I was growing up, I was told to get good grades, study hard, and get a good job. So I did the best I could, but I started slow.

I felt challenges almost everywhere I turned.
Couldn't figure out girls.
Couldn't figure out good grades.
Couldn't figure out friends.

The facts about my start in academia: I had a 2.8 GPA, was rejected on my first application to a state school, and got a 21 on the ACT—below average. Because of my low ACT, I had to apply twice to get accepted into Iowa State University.

I thought I was destined for a doomed existence. I thought something was wrong with me (most days I still do). Life was hard for me. I was diagnosed with ADHD in 7th grade—and that was back in the 90s when it was difficult to get diagnosed. The testing process wasn't enjoyable.

When I graduated from college, after getting fired from an internship, I moved home to start my first business from my parents' basement (in their toy closet), but things were bleak.

The business started slowly, and I wasn't making much money. I remember being in a Game Stop looking at Guitar Hero 2 for Playstation 2. I looked at it with longing because I couldn't buy it; I only had $123 to my name.

Every day I woke up to work on my business, I worked to fight against my own sense of inadequacy. After a while, it started working but primarily because I focused on a deep transformation inside my brain.

It took me two years.
The good news is that you'll get it even faster with this book.

My first year in business I made $8,000, my second year I made $27,000, my third year I made $120,000, my fourth year I made $360,000—and my yearly income has continued to grow since. I have started sixteen businesses, failed at eleven, and succeeded with five of them. My best idea took three years to build before I stepped away. Three businesses are still running today.

But the most important part of all of this is that building these businesses was a ton of fun.

I found the patterns and ways of thinking that made me successful time and time again.

Fast forward to the present day, and I have a zero-hour work week with a fully self-managed business from which I collect passive distributions. The business has a CEO, it grows without me, and I collect 25% of the profits. It does over two million dollars per year in revenue with a wonderful margin for me. A few people have offered me $6,000,000 for the business, but I have declined.

Here's why some have offered me as much as six million.

> Business type: Software as a service.
> New Monthly Customers: ~30 sign-ups
> Average Monthly Revenue Per Customer: ~$145
> Monthly Revenue: ~$185,000 (average revenue from Q3 2019)
> Monthly Churn: 0.7 percent
> Net New Accounts Each Month: 20

The CHURN numbers put this business in a top category among SaaS. You see we have 20 new accounts each month after losing our customers, so the business grows by $2,900 every single month (20 x 145).

I have a very nice life because of this business. It is very stable and over 10 years old. Not dependent on Google slaps or Facebook ads or the wind blowing over your Amazon store.

To prove to myself that this wasn't an accident, I started teaching people the same process I followed to see if it would work. We have created 15 millionaires in four to five years time and hundreds of success stories in the six-figure range. Many of them employees. All of them started from zero.

I recorded 15 of their transformational stories in this book.

We live in a world where new books are created faster than ever. The more knowledge is created and shared, the more important it becomes to find "source-level" stuff. Blueprints, concepts, and ideas that you learn once but can apply in 100 different situations.

This is the little book with "source-level" knowledge about what it truly takes to start from scratch. I've been writing it in my mind for over a decade.

I wrote this book to impart my knowledge so that entrepreneurship could be made accessible to everyone. The knowledge here has given me my own freedom. Please read it and find your own freedom too.

## The Most Important Question of All...
## Easily Forgotten

"Hey, Dane, I know it's your day off after working all week, but can you come in today? Bring in your laptop and all of your things, OK?"

"Oh sure. Are we doing some last-minute work?"

"Just bring in your things, OK?"

My heart sank... *What could they possibly want at 3:00 p.m. on a Friday? I* thought. *They had all day to call me; why wait till the last minute on a Friday?*

"Fire Dane." I was last on the to-do list that day.

With one week left in my internship.

I got this call back when I was in Minnesota at Ernst & Young. I had that Friday off, and I was getting ready for an amazing weekend with my father and my friends, who were all coming down to wakeboard to celebrate my last week of work.

I was humiliated. I didn't like that feeling.

The request to come in with my laptop was the opening volley in my termination.

I was so caught off guard I cried in front of the Human Resources woman when she let me go... That was embarrassing. I had one week left in my internship. "I can't go to Disney and finish the internship? There's just one week left!" I pleaded. "I want to spend time with my co-workers for one more week."

"Don't worry, Dane. You'll be a great fit somewhere else. We liked your performance; you're just not a good fit here, and now that we know that, we don't think it would be a good idea to send you to Disney."

My intern friends all completed their internships with a final week on-site at Disney down in Florida. They did a shot in my honor and sent a text saying, "We miss you man!" Even though it was well-meaning, the text hurt. I wanted to be there. It was a hard week. I was so embarrassed to have my father hear the news when he came to pick me up.

On that day a silent vengeance filled my heart without my direct awareness. This was the day the seed for entrepreneurship was planted.

*I wanted control over my 9-to-5 life.*

"I will never be fired again," I told myself.

As painful as that experience was, I'm extremely grateful for it.

I'm so happy I don't work there (or anywhere else, for that matter). Being an employee was a terrible experience for me. Especially being an auditor. You show up early, stay late, and people still don't like you. And why would they? You're looking up their backside and asking for documents all day.

The truth was they fired me after I spoke up at a company dinner and said some...things.

I was sitting next to a young employee who had a wedding ring on his finger.
"You're married," I said.
"Yes."

I thought to myself, *This job requires a lot of travel. I wonder how much he sees his wife.*
"How often do you get to see your wife?"

He said, "One week per month on average we get to be with each other."
"Just one week!?" I exclaimed. "Why?"

"Well, she works for another auditing firm, so if she's gone, I'm home, and if I'm home, she's usually gone."

Now I don't know about you, but this made me terribly sad and scared the crap out of me. I thought to myself, *How could anyone ever be happy doing this?*

With an earnest heart, as we were all out at dinner, I looked around to the table, and they didn't look authentically happy to me. *Maybe they choose to be OK with what they were given?*

I got the chance to work next to a partner that day; those are the highest-paid people, who everyone respects and wants to be.

Apparently once you hit partner, that's when life gets good. That's what we are sold anyway.

I wanted to be a partner too until I sat next to one.

The partner cold called Fortune 500 companies all day and sold accounting services.

*This is what I'm looking forward to?*

There was no way I could go on here.

I couldn't help myself... I looked around at the table and asked, "Is anybody happy at this job?"

The question was honest and showed my vulnerability.

I wasn't happy. I was eating candy and drinking caffeine everyday at 2:00 p.m. just to get through the rest of the day. I wanted to jump from my cubicle. I hated myself at that job.

*The highest level of promotion includes cold calling.*

*A married man sees his wife one week a month.*

The thoughts were racing through my mind. Then I was brought back to reality when someone answered...

"I'm really happy here, Dane," said one of the seniors at the company.

"Really?" I asked. "Why?"

"Because I get to do something new every day."

"Well, what did you do today?"

It turned out his answer was the same thing I had done that day. And what I did that day sucked.

At the company dinner I wanted to genuinely know if anyone was happy. Needless to say, asking that question did not have the effect I wanted. No one else spoke up. They all kept their jobs, and I was fired the very next day.

They sent the message loud and clear to me and all their employees when I was fired: Do not question the system.

Because of that, I decided I would never let anyone control my destiny.

And by 29 years old, I was set. I never had to work again, and I did it by following what I outline in this book.

I tell you this story because all of my success started when I was honest with myself and asked the single most important question, "Am I actually happy?" My success did not start because I'm special or talented. It started because I was honest.

I think many of the auditors I worked with would crush it in business if they had the proper training. I recognized their entrepreneurial souls, stuck like cogs in a wheel.

But I digress... Let's get you some results. Please send Ernst and Young your thanks for setting me free. I am truly grateful for the day I was fired.

Let's get to it!

# WHAT YOU DO & DON'T NEED

This is business in a nutshell.

Customer → Uses A Mechanism → To Get A Result

Forget this and die a slow and painful death.

Now here is where it gets dicey.

The new entrepreneur obsesses about the mechanism. And I mean they are obsessed. It has to be shiny and new, sexy and creative, and never done before.

Most think, *"who am I to create a mechanism worth paying for?"*

I don't create the mechanisms. I hire those out. The very thing that stops most people from getting into business... I outsourced. I hire out the creation of the mechanisms.

My focus is on a customer and the result they want. The mechanisms could be infinite.

You think that to be in business you need to find your idea or your mechanism first, that the mechanism is what prevents you from playing in business, that you need a golden idea to move forward.

No.

In truth the customer doesn't care about the mechanism. They want a result.

This is excellent news. Because it levels the playing field.

You can be 15 years old or 80.

You can be a boy or a girl.

You can be a dropout or a graduate.

The only thing you need is to deliver a result.

And you can outsource the delivery of the result. That's actually what most business owners do.

I spoke to a 15-year-old teenager the other day with a youthful voice who's building a product to teach golfers how to improve their golf game. Here's what he told me.

"Yeah, no one wants to listen to a 15-year-old kid teach, so I found a top golf pro and asked them to teach it for me, and I'm giving him a percentage."

Even a 15 year old can hire out the mechanism.

You don't need any of the things people say you do.

You don't need an idea...

Or money...

Or experience...

Or even confidence when you start...

All you need is to generate a result for someone. Now turn the page and prepare for the journey of a lifetime. Because entrepreneurship is so much better than what people have told you.

# CHAPTER 1:

# FIRST, WHAT YOU DON'T NEED TO START A BUSINESS

---

*"Everyday I woke up to work for someone else, I felt like a piece of me died."*
— The trapped employee.

This section will show you what it's like to start a business without getting into Harvard (only to drop out like Bill Gates and Mark Zuckerberg), without putting yourself or your family at risk, and without a lot of self esteem.

*Here's the bottom line:* Entrepreneurs are not better or smarter than you, and many of them are just as risk averse as an employee.

Allow me to demonstrate. Let's start with the first concept.

## Why you don't need to be a genius or an expert

Not only do you not need to be the expert. You don't want to be. Being an expert can often hurt your chances of success because it automatically focuses you on details that don't move a business forward.

Experts don't usually make great entrepreneurs, yet most of them try to be one.

Carl was an expert. He was an employee for Tesla Motors. But he wanted out.

At the time I met him he was also quiet and shy.

He did epic stuff there. He designed the interface for their vehicles and the company website check out process. The stuff at Tesla looks gorgeous.

That was Carl.

Yet with all that skill, he still didn't know how to start his own business.

But if we fast forward to today, he has quit Tesla. He's a multi-millionaire. He's confident. He's very happy. He even leads a team of people that report to him.

If you want to have full freedom, you don't want to be the expert; you want to be the *owner*.

You'll need to get out of the metaphorical car that says expert, and get into the one that says owner.

This car has a different motor, a different transmission, and will take you time to learn how to drive, because being an owner is a completely different set of skills you were never taught.

Carl had all the things others say make you happy. He worked close to the CEO, had excellent benefits, and worked in the famous Silicon Valley. But he knew he wasn't happy.

You could say it's because he didn't have freedom, he didn't have all the money he wanted, he had to go into work every day. But Carl loved working. That's not why he wasn't happy.

Here's why Carl was unhappy; He was waking up to build someone else's dream, not his.

For most entrepreneurs, it's not about the money. It's about building your own dreams instead of working on someone else's while having full control over your own time and schedule.

**How did Carl do it?**

By transforming.

To start, he needed proper business 101 training. He needed to find someone with a problem to build a business around. So he started talking to business owners and asking them questions to *find the pain*. He asked them a powerful question, "What do you use Microsoft Excel for in your business?"

Then he sat back and listened.

Microsoft Excel is a hotbed for potential products because companies use it to cobble together solutions for their various business needs. (There are many questions you can ask to find the pain, which you will learn later in this book. This is just one example question.) One particular business owner was using Excel to track important financial metrics across four different locations in their industry. The resulting setup was pretty archaic.

Then Carl asked a second question, "How does that process work for you right now?" This question put the business owner in story mode and allowed Carl to really connect with the issue by hearing the dirty details of the problem.

The owner said, "It's really hard because we have different versions of spreadsheets that have the wrong information and employees mistakenly modify them however they want. We don't have strict permissions for certain fields."

So then Carl asked, "What would your dream solution be?"

The owner said, "I'd love one central location with the proper permissions so that I could see all my data at a glance. Also, I would just use Quickbooks, but I need a few more fields than they will allow to directly match my business needs."

Wonderful insights.

Now Carl has a new business idea. Did he get it from being an expert? No. He got it from helping someone else and knowing the questions to ask.

He didn't come up with either the problem or the solution. His customer just told him both.

So he had an idea; what next?

## Summary for Why You Don't Have to Be a Genius:

Instead of Carl being an expert or genius and looking at what he knew, he looked out into the world and asked someone about their problems instead.

Most of us seek the path of trying to be competent and knowledgeable enough to start a business. Instead, focus on learning about a problem experienced by another human; you'll figure out the rest naturally.

It can be scary and vulnerable to ask these questions when you don't know what you're doing.

In a later section you'll learn exactly how to follow this process.

## Why you don't need money;

Now Carl had his new idea...for a software product in this case...but he needed to get it built.

How?

Carl told a developer from work about his new idea. The developer loved it, saying, "Dude, you have an idea that someone wants to pay for before it's even built? That's awesome. I'll build it for you." Carl tried to pay him, but the developer said, "No, don't pay me up now. Instead, I want 10% of the future revenues."

Carl continued working full-time while his product was being built by someone else.

As for the user interface design, instead of hiring someone else to do that work and giving them another 10% of the future revenues, he did that part himself. But he could have hired that out as well.

Did he need money to start? No. He just needed to ask questions and then find an expert to create a solution.

In this case, he met his developer at work. But a quick Google search for "find a reliable software developer" will return plenty of sites with Amazon.com-type reviews for developers you can trust.

What is Carl's risk so far?

He didn't come up with an idea.
He didn't write code for his product.
He didn't use any money.

Instead he needed to be an expert at finding pain. Then he put an expert in place once the problem had been defined and articulated.

So, is entrepreneurship risky? Being trained in entrepreneurship creates safety. It's being uneducated that is risky. Please remember that.

Some say, "It takes money to make money." And the thing is this is a true statement for an untrained, uneducated brain. What you really need is a new vision for how businesses can be built from nothing. Once you have that vision, you can start an endless number of ideas from scratch without financial risk.

And also, as you get into this book, it's important to remember this process works no matter what product idea you find. You could find the pain for stay-at-home moms, eye doctors, or children learning the piano. (One of our graduates discovered a problem where younger children couldn't reach the keys to the piano because they were not tall enough, and so they needed a piano pillow to boost them up to reach it. A great, simple pain that isn't software.)

### Summary for Why You Don't Need Money:

Have you ever heard of Kickstarter.com? They raise money for products before they are built. Pre-selling is normal nowadays. You don't need money to get started; you need a solvable problem someone would pay for.

Steve Jobs didn't have money when he started Apple, so he gave stock options and sought investors.

But I don't like getting investment capital. In this example, Carl didn't pay anything to build his software product; he had it built for free. And I didn't spend any of my money to build my first few products; I got money from my customers.

If you take the time to build your brain, you won't need to rely on money to get started. You'll be able to start from scratch once you learn the process in this book.

## Why you don't need 12-hour days;

Carl continued to work at Tesla full time while he started his business on the side. He devoted 1.5 hours a day to his business in the mornings and after six months, he had a $4,000-per-month business.

Five years later, he has a multi-million dollar company.

He didn't leave his job to start the new business. He left once he was safe.

Here's how he did it.

Carl lives in California, which is in the Pacific time zone. He would wake up at 6:00 a.m. each morning and talk to business owners on the East Coast, where it was 9:00 a.m. (three hours later). He did this all on purpose. He'd call up businesses and send emails, asking the owners about their painful problems for an hour and a half each morning. After two months, he had five really good ideas to pick from. He reviewed his ideas and picked the easiest and most profitable idea to build.

He'd send messages like this: "Hey there! I'm contacting a group of business owners to ask them about the really painful problems they face. My intention is to build a new business around a real problem instead of guessing. What sort of painful problems do you face on a day-to-day basis that you wish could be removed?"

Only a few emails would get him a great reply; a few would say "no thanks." Most of the time, no one responded. Carl took so much action so fast, sometimes he would call the same business twice on accident.

"Uhm, you just called us a minute ago."

"Oh, sorry," Carl would say, and then he'd hang up and move on.

It didn't matter what responses he got. Nothing would stop him. What mattered is he moved like a freight train.

I told Carl he could be more kind to himself. That he didn't have to subject himself to all that rejection from the massive action he was taking. That there were gentler ways to do this.

Gentler ways that I teach and follow myself.

I asked Carl why he didn't just stick to email because there is less rejection there, and he told me he would only cold call when he ran out of emails to send, but he made sure to take an hour and a half of action every morning no matter what.

That's it. That's all he needed to do in the morning. Then he could turn his brain off for the rest of the day and focus on his job.

But the first thing he did each morning was work on his dream.

That's an enormously powerful act of self-love—putting your own dream first. For an entrepreneur at heart, it can be pretty painful to work on someone else's dream (instead of building your own).

Carl told me, "everyday I woke up to work for someone else, I felt like a piece of me died."

But he was stuck on how to start until he learned this process.

We are taught that you need to work 12-hour days to become an entrepreneur and start a business. But starting is a matter of doing the critical tasks that don't waste time. Once you know what those are, you can start with a couple of hours a day.

## Summary for Why You Don't Need 12 Hour Days

If you focus on the critical actions, you only need two hours a day to start a business.

If you can devote the first two hours of your morning or the evening (or two hours during the day) to your new idea, you can get started building a business. Just like Carl did.

It can feel so difficult to start, so scary to do something new. Later, we'll clear through the identity, the fear, and the thoughts that stop you.

# Why Hard Work Isn't Enough;

Carl had a tremendously difficult time starting his business. Not because of the tactics—but because of his emotions. He held so much stress in his system that he could not sleep unless he took ice baths.

He worked hard, and that moved him forward, but it was taxing his system. He had a fearlessness towards his actions and it was running his body ragged. The hard work gave him results and confidence, but his inner world was falling apart.

Then he learned about the significant power of limiting beliefs. He took one full day to work on all of his limiting beliefs and transformed them using a four-question process called The Work by Byron Katie (find it free online and give it a shot).

One by one, Carl went through all of his beliefs and addressed each of them. Beliefs like: *Business is hard. Making money is difficult. This is supposed to be hard. This can't be easy. I'm not good enough to succeed. I'm too shy. I'm an introvert.*

He transformed each of them—one by one.

Carl stopped taking ice baths and slept well again, just by rewiring his beliefs. What happened was he transformed his identity from employee to entrepreneur slowly.

He had to transform thoughts and beliefs to move forward.

The powerful thing is that it took one full day to shift his biggest blocks, and he's been working on his beliefs consistently since. Transformation like this can sometimes provide a big quick hit, but then hard work over time to really sink in.

We'll get into the "how-to" of transformation later on in this book.

It's simple and straightforward.

## Summary for Why Hard Work Isn't Enough

Burnout will happen if you try and fight your own beliefs. You will lose. You need the proper tools to work with beliefs so they are cleared. Take the time to reverse and clear them so you can move forward with freedom.

Use *"The DJP Framework"* to quickly clear through your blocks for free at StartFromZero.com/Yes. Yes it's free, no email capture required.

You might be thinking, *But, Dane! This is only one example! What if it doesn't apply to me?!*

In the example above, Carl used Start From Zero Thinking to make a digital software product, but the same process can be applied to any kind of product.

Let me give you another quick example of what's possible with an online course. They are much simpler to build, but the process is the same. To get started, we need to identify a painful problem that can be solved. Personally, I started by observing the people around me. I noticed that many of them had issues completing their goals.

And they were in pain from it.

For example, they'd write down a new goal down, but it would never come to fruition.

It looked like they were having issues with their mental chatter. People were getting defeated by it.
You've seen this happen before, right?

When I noticed this problem, I tried to solve it myself...but then I realized I wasn't an expert at it. I started having personal limiting beliefs come up. I thought, *Who am I to be teaching about mindset? I've still got my own issues. Who am I to be representing what it's like to have a healthy mind?*

Oops.

"Back up, Dane," I told myself. "You don't need to know everything."

Then I remembered what I teach. *Things don't have to be perfect to move forward, and I don't need to be an expert. I can hire out my insecurities.* So instead of trying to solve this problem on my own, I focused on understanding the pain more first.

To do that, I wrote a Facebook post that said, "Does anyone here struggle with any mindset issues? I'm thinking about making a course on this. Send me a private message or comment below—I'd like to chat with you."

Five people reached out. I got brave and asked them about their mindset issues—I was nervous that people wouldn't want to talk about something so personal. I'd say, "Thanks for contacting me. What are your current problems with mindset that you'd like to change?"

I was surprised. All of them were willing to be vulnerable, and all of them said the same thing: "I need help focusing."

Whoa. That was awesome. I was shocked to hear how clear everyone was on their main issue, and that it was the same for all of them. They knew what the problem was right away. And it was just one word.

Focus.

Now I was not a focus expert but I knew someone who was. I went to this person and said, "Hey, will you teach a course on mindset around focus and procrastination? To help people reach their goals? I'll give you 20% of the profits, and all you have to do is show up and teach. You won't have to do marketing, sales, website creation, or advertising. I'll handle all of that. You just focus on teaching."

This expert said, "Yes."

In a short while, I had found someone to help my new customers with their pain.

Once I had my expert, I sold a 12-week mindset course to these customers. We called the first version of the course, "What's In The Way Is The Way: A Counterintuitive Approach to a Squeaky Clean Mind."

I went to my list of interested people and told them, "Hey, I've got an expert who can help with focusing. We are going to teach a 12-week course to solve this problem for you. Are you interested?"

The original four out of five people purchased it. Which was really good.

We still had no product built. No website. No logo. No business plan. No location. But we did risk a little of our time.

Before each weekly training, I'd meet with the expert and interview them on what he or she wanted to teach for the week. I'd document the interview and turn it into a PowerPoint. Then we'd present it as a team.

I was the steward of this business and brought it to life. That's it. I wasn't trying to show off, be impressive, or build my resume. I was trying to solve a problem.

And now...we have customers who are free to focus. We have results, happier people, and another income stream.

Can you see what would have happened if I had let my own thoughts stop me from making this course? It would have never happened!

This process can be so mind-blowing for people at first. They just don't get how simple it is. Let me recap what happened here:

I found a problem: Mindset.
I got to the deeper issue: Focus.

I found an expert who knew how to fix the problem; paid them 20% of profits.

I sold the course before we created it.

We created and recorded the course on the fly.

Now I have a sellable product that I own.
Now I have an asset producing regular income.
Now the expert has a passive income stream.
Now the customers can focus.

Everybody wins. And I get a chance to taste even more freedom.

Now you might be asking, "How do you acquire the skills to do all of this?" That's what I'll be teaching you in the coming chapters.

So, that is the great "secret." You connect with another human and listen to them. Once you've done that, you find and put experts in place to solve their problems and share the revenue. If you can do that, you'll be set for life.

And because our society is full of people who want to be experts, you'll always be able to find these people and hire them. And because most experts don't truly want ownership, you'll be in a position of power.

This kind of ownership thinking is a different way of reasoning than we are taught. It will probably feel foreign at first.

You don't have to be an expert anymore. You just need to find painful problems and solve them for others. Think of entrepreneurship more like being a detective and a problem solver.

Welcome to freedom. You can do this.

*If you want it.*

In this chapter, we covered the things you don't need.

You don't have to be a genius or an expert, you don't need money, you don't need 12-hour days, and you need to work hard *and* delete false beliefs. The rest of this book is full of meat on how these results can be accomplished in various situations.

Now that you see it's possible to start something on the side with limited time, no money, and no product ideas, let's get you some results.

# CHAPTER 2:

# SECOND, WHAT YOU DO NEED TO START A BUSINESS

Who is entrepreneurship *really* for? Many try entrepreneurship only to get beaten down into failure. I want to stop that from happening by showing you some data.

What are the personality attributes of a successful entrepreneur?

## The Statistics of Our Top Entrepreneur Graduates

I consulted with Dr. Douglas J. Tataryn, who decided to run an analysis on our most successful graduates in order to find their commonalities. I thought this was a brilliant idea. He thought that when we discovered the commonalities, we could use this information to groom even more successful entrepreneurs.

First we had to find a personality assessment that was more descriptive and comprehensive than Myers Briggs or StrengthsFinder. We wanted something specific. We found something called Hexaco.

Hexaco is an academic personality assessment you've probably never heard of because it was created by academics. And we liked it because we needed precise details. Hexaco is an analysis of your personality across 26 different factors, including honesty, humility, anxiety, fearfulness, diligence, organization etc.

I contacted 30 entrepreneurs (many of them my own graduates) who qualified as successful in business and/or were financially free. It was an undertaking to wrangle all of these busy entrepreneurs. It took 90 days and a bunch of follow-ups to get the 30 assessments back from these successful folks.

We then built software to crawl these results and organize the data into a master spreadsheet. Then we crunched the numbers. Through statistical analysis, we found the top five highest scoring traits and also the bottom five lowest scoring traits.

The most exciting thing that we discovered is that the top five and bottom five traits can be shifted or improved, which means it is possible to build the brain of an entrepreneur no matter who you are. With laser-like precision, you can see the top five personality traits we found and work to remove the bottom five.

Before I share the data, I just need to say I have a great fear you will look at this and instantly come to a dismal conclusion about your chances of success as an entrepreneur.

First, please note that this is not how all entrepreneurs are; this only a sample of 30 entrepreneurs who have the freedom to work when and how they want. Some are millionaires; some make $60,000 a year as stay-at-home moms.

**But all have time freedom.**

They all have the skills to build financial freedom. Many of them can build businesses from scratch. Some of them build passive real estate portfolios.

Again, all of them work by choice and have time freedom.

If you have yet to be successful, you might be able to identify one of the traits that you are missing.

The top five traits we discovered in order of importance are:

1. Creativity.
2. Social Self-Esteem.
3. Diligence.
4. Fairness.
5. Altruism.

As we look at these, it's clear to see how helpful these would be in building a business. This is a wonderful list of traits.

Creativity means you like to innovate and experiment. Social self-esteem means you can initiate conversations. Diligence means you work hard. Fairness means you have integrity in deals. Altruism means you have consideration for all parties in a transaction, even the ones not directly involved.

All of these traits could be built with focus.

Don't consider yourself creative? Creativity can be built. Pick up a book on creativity and practice the exercises inside. Look up creativity books on Amazon and find a 5-star book.

Not outgoing with high social self-esteem? Join Toastmasters in your area and practice public speaking. To get started just Google "toastmasters in my [city]."

Aren't diligent? Don't work hard? You might be surprised. Most people I know love working hard when they know with certainty they are going to get rich and help people.

Would you have thought fairness and altruism would be on there? Indeed, an entrepreneur won't make it very far if they are missing these traits.

Entrepreneurs who cut corners or treat people unfairly do not last. And if they do, it's rare. And they are usually hated.

You don't want to be hated.

# Remember You Can Be Yourself as an Entrepreneur...

One of my friends is a very successful entrepreneur, and yet he did not score high on one of these traits. So guess what he does? He hires that trait out. That's what many entrepreneurs do very well—they find their weak points and they get support.

The heart of an entrepreneur can't be stopped by anything.

Entrepreneurship is amazing because it's one field you can really build around who you are. You don't have to change. With that being said I found these qualities incredibly helpful for focusing on getting a business off the ground.

## Modeling Benjamin Franklin

Benjamin Franklin was famous for building his personality by working on one trait at a time. For example, for a period of weeks he might pick "diligence" as the trait he wanted to learn, and he'd find the right books and practice diligence.

But...he'd *only* focus on diligence.

Now...let's look at the five traits they scored the lowest on.

The traits they had low scores on in order were...

1. Fearfulness
2. Anxiety
3. Dependence

4.  Greed Avoidance
5.  Perfectionism

This was deeply inspiring for me to see. I believe entrepreneurship is possible for you, if you take time to take care of these traits. I also believe there are always exceptions to the rule.

Most of these traits can be nurtured with proper therapy, coaching, or training. You can have healthy fearfulness and healthy anxiety. With the proper healing of past trauma you can heal a strong need for dependence or perfectionism.

Most items on this list are obvious. You'd want to score low on fearfulness, anxiety, dependence, and perfectionism.

Low fearfulness means you don't avoid feeling harmed.

Low anxiety means you don't sweat every single detail as much and focus on the important stuff.

Low dependence means you can handle many problems on your own.

Low perfectionism means you can launch a product or write an email without it being perfect.

But what is greed avoidance? It is exactly as it sounds. If you score high, you avoid expressing wealth outwardly. If you score low, you enjoy expressing your wealth. I laughed out loud when I saw this because of how awesome it is. This finding means this group of entrepreneurs aren't shy about expressing their wealth in their own authentic way. Whether it's the purchase of a Tesla, a high rise, or a ballin' Mercedes Twin Diesel V8. It means that they enjoy their wealth authentically. Which is a perfectly healthy thing to do.

Even though this is a small sample size of 30 entrepreneurs, in my 10 years of experience in business and in mentoring over 1,200 humans,

I've found relating to these traits in a healthy way greatly improves an entrepreneur's success.

If you've been trying entrepreneurship for years, and have really wanted this, you can do it. Take time to build the top five traits until you have them. And take time to reduce the bottom five so they don't run your life anymore.

There's a book called SNAP: How To Change Your Personality In 30 Days, which will help.

Just so you are clear on what to work on and what to avoid, here is how Hexaco defines each category.

The Creativity scale assesses one's preference for innovation and experiment. Low scorers have little inclination for original thought, whereas high scorers actively seek new solutions to problems and express themselves in art.

The Social Self-Esteem scale assesses a tendency to have positive self-regard, particularly in social contexts. High scorers are generally satisfied with themselves and consider themselves to have likable qualities, whereas low scorers tend to have a sense of personal worthlessness and to see themselves as unpopular.

The Diligence scale assesses a tendency to work hard. Low scorers have little self-discipline and are not strongly motivated to achieve, whereas high scorers have a strong "work ethic" and are willing to exert themselves.

The Fairness scale assesses a tendency to avoid fraud and corruption. Low scorers are willing to gain by cheating or stealing, whereas high scorers are unwilling to take advantage of other individuals or of society at large.

The Altruism (versus Antagonism) scale assesses a tendency to be sympathetic and soft-hearted toward others. High scorers avoid causing harm and react with generosity toward those who are weak or in need of help, whereas low scorers are not upset by the prospect of hurting others and may be seen as hard-hearted.

The Fearfulness scale assesses a tendency to experience fear. Low scorers feel little fear of injury and are relatively tough, brave, and insensitive to physical pain, whereas high scorers are strongly inclined to avoid physical harm.

The Anxiety scale assesses a tendency to worry in a variety of contexts. Low scorers feel little stress in response to difficulties, whereas high scorers tend to become preoccupied even by relatively minor problems.

The Dependence scale assesses one's need for emotional support from others. Low scorers feel self-assured and able to deal with problems without any help or advice, whereas high scorers want to share their difficulties with those who will provide encouragement and comfort.

The Greed Avoidance scale assesses a tendency to be uninterested in possessing lavish wealth, luxury goods, and signs of high social status. Low scorers want to enjoy and to display wealth and privilege, whereas high scorers are not especially motivated by monetary or social-status considerations.

The Perfectionism scale assesses a tendency to be thorough and concerned with details. Low scorers tolerate some errors in their work and tend to neglect details, whereas high scorers check carefully for mistakes and potential improvements.

## ⸺Find out Where You Are Right Now ⸺

Visit Hexaco.org and take the free test. It's one hundred or so questions. When you get your results back, look at how you compare to those of our successful entrepreneurs. Upload and share your results with our Start From Zero online community at StartFromZero.com/Yes.

You'll want to see lower than average scores for...

1. Fearfulness
2. Anxiety
3. Dependence
4. Greed Avoidance
5. Perfectionism

You'll want to see higher than average scores for...

1. Creativity
2. Social Self Esteem
3. Diligence
4. Fairness
5. Altruism

## Make the Change or Hire What You Need to Succeed

Once you identify which high score traits or low score traits need some work, you can go to work on them or hire them out.

**Catch yourself saying:** "Oh shoot, now I see I can never be a successful entrepreneur. I don't have social self-esteem or creativity." This list does not have to define you. It's a small sample size, and we have exceptions to this data inside the Halls of Transformation, where you'll get to meet 15 entrepreneurs and see their top five and bottom five Hexaco scores individually.

These traits are helpful to have and to develop, but not scoring well on them doesn't have to stop you.

# Here's Why I'm Telling You This

All of the tactics in the world won't help if you're highly perfectionistic and highly fearful. You've got to solve those problems at the root.

Ultimately, I want to remind you of self-acceptance. Nothing is wrong with who you are. This is not a list to look at to then discover your own secret worthlessness. This is a list to empower you to see what might be needed.

Many of us are walking around wondering if we are worthy of our dream. This list shows you how to increase the chances of success for your dream!

Remember, these are only qualities and they are not who you are. Please be sure to love yourself enough to notice when you're making an excuse and don't change anything you really love about yourself. Success as an entrepreneur can be possible in all cases.

But now you know some helpful data.

## You Can Do So Much Good

Entrepreneurship is glorious because of the level of service and profit you can bring to the entire world. I want to show you the heart of entrepreneurship, which I believe is to Start From Zero, no matter your circumstances.

I happen to be another one of those "privileged, middle class, white males" who used these principles. But I've taught these same skills to people of various races, colors, intelligence levels, and incomes. I've seen immigrants and people with terrible English and thick accents apply the same process, and it worked.

This will work for you if you want it too.

What needs to happen for success is a deep transformation in the brain, while building the proper structures of entrepreneurship at the same time.

## Are You Ready to Move?

If I were to give you a $100,000-per-month business right now, would you be able to run it?

If I were to give you a $10,000-per-month business, would you know how to handle that?

No.

Unless you'd been trained. You wouldn't.

So instead of only desiring an outcome, also wish to transform into the kind of person who *can* handle that type of outcome. If you become that kind of person, you'll not only be able to handle it, you can create the same outcome over and over again.

## This is the great secret.

In order to achieve this transformation, we need to work with your mind in two areas. Identity and beliefs. These are critical.

No tactic in the world is going to help you if your mind is programmed against your desires.

What you need is a deep transformation like Carl or Juliana or Cris or Dave. You'll hear their stories in the halls of transformation later on. These graduates are all capable of making millions.

That's life-changing dough.

And if it was all taken away, they could build it back up because of who they are internally. But the key is the transformation to do that.

And that's what you need. To transform.

If you are not wealthy or if you don't feel free right now, let's start there.

# CHAPTER 3:

# DEEPLY PROGRAM THE BEST THOUGHTS

**Heads up:** This section can be threatening to the mind in its current form. You've been warned.

Would you like to build wealth and freedom in an automatic way without having to think or try so hard?

It's possible.

We can do that by programming the unconscious with great thoughts.

For you to become financially abundant and free, you will need to bring in a new set of beliefs to operate by.

This can be *very confrontational.*

Let me explain.

I will challenge the belief system around being an employee. For example, let's say I told you that being an employee is risky and being an entrepreneur is safe.

How does that make you feel?

> Employee = risk.
> Entrepreneur = safe.

Take a deep breath.

Literally just take a quick deep breath.

What comes up for you? For most of us, it doesn't compute. The automatic response is to reject it. Maybe even to hate this idea. You might say, "what?!" That's OK. When you reject this concept, that is your belief system in action.

It is not right or wrong (although your belief system thinks it is right). It is simply reacting to how it has been programmed.

You've been programmed to have certain beliefs.

I'm not asking you to abandon this belief. This is an invitation to a new way of thinking.

To my mind, safety in entrepreneurship is a truth because of how I've built my brain. But I had to make the transformation first.

Here's what I believe about being an employee:

- If you stop working, your income stops: *risky*.
- Most employees have one stream of income: *risky*.
- I could be fired or let go because of a company merger or other circumstances: *risky*.
- If something bad happens to me, I can't work, and my family is without an income: *risky*.
- My income has a ceiling, and someone else dictates it: *low control*.
- I am reliant on someone else for my financial future: *low control*.
- You get taxed on all of your income before you spend it: *low control*.

Then you have the other annoying factors like not being in charge of your own promotions. You compete against co-workers for positions. Being an employee doesn't allow you to set up legacy wealth for your family.

Today entrepreneurship methodologies are so well tested it has become more science than chance. Because of these new methodologies, I believe that being an employee is extremely risky, and if you have a family, and you are an employee, I believe you must build a skill set to fall back on if you're fired.

If you like being an employee, I am not saying that you should leave your job. I'm telling you that you need to build more than one stream of income. Don't depend on exchanging time for money for your livelihood. Take the time to learn how to be an entrepreneur, just as you took the time to be an employee.

Once you are trained and practiced, you can approach entrepreneurship safely.

When many people want to make more money, they will get a second job or fire up the equivalent of Uber or Lyft. But that requires you to spend more of your valuable time.

If you want more money, don't exchange more time by getting a second job. Take the time to build your income stream brain instead.

Now... let's check in...

How did you feel reading this? Did any of it feel threatening? Did you have objections to what I wrote? Did your mind want to fight me at any point? That's your belief system arguing with mine.

Now the question is...

Does your belief system support your desire to get wealthy, or does it keep you stuck somewhere else? I encourage you to consciously choose a belief system that supports the vision you want for your life.

These upcoming sections are about how to wake up from faulty thoughts and beliefs.

This discussion about entrepreneurship vs. employment is just one small example of how threatening it can be to choose a new belief system. Be gentle with yourself, go slow, and undertake this process with care.

# CHAPTER 4

# INSPIRE YOUR OWN HEART

(Welcome! Not to fear. There is a process you can follow to make this section easier).

**This is the highest leverage work you can do in just two hours.**

Most of us avoid doing this layer of reflection, and then we keep failing over and over again. If you'd like to finally succeed and end the cycle, face this section first.

Right now.

Today.

It'll take you two hours. And you can do just about anything for two hours.

First, we need to make our behaviors automatic.

**So, We Declare Deeply.**

## Here's How to Make The Declaration to Yourself & Those Who Encourage You.

There is a way in which you can make a declaration that roots down within you so deep, everything in your life will organize around it.

You won't have to fight yourself in the same way.

Writing down your heart's true desire can feel so difficult...that we can't even do it. If you can't write it down because it's too unknown or scary, that's OK. Don't rush this. You can go slow. The more difficult it is, the more it usually matters to you.

Resistance is a positive indicator, not a bad one.

This declaration needs to be for you first and foremost.

When it comes to your declaration, other people might make fun of you, which could really hurt. Your dream is tender in the beginning and needs love and protection. The need for approval is a sneaky thing. When you're able to, write it down, read it to yourself, keep it to yourself, and then share it only those you know will encourage you.

For the other folks in your life, let them see what you wrote down after you've started living it.

"What do I want to do for myself?" is a good starting point.

This stuff is best done gently so you're not frazzled. Gentle change tends to be permanent change. This realization can be disheartening at first because it means we have to be present with a lot of discomfort while we grow and change.

But it's the path that creates permanent effects.

Wouldn't you rather just do the work once and be done anyway?

You might be thinking, *just give me the "easy" button, damnit!*

Well, this is the easy button. You just have to build it yourself. But it will be your button and only yours. You can push it anytime you want...once you've transformed.

And it gets easier. Much easier. My advice is to be gentle so the change is permanent. My experience shows that it takes around two years to completely update your brain to this new world of entrepreneurship and build that button. You can accelerate things greatly, but you can't frantically jump ahead without sacrificing an inner confidence. It will bite you in the butt.

## Making The Declaration:

The first step in making the declaration is to breathe self-worth and value into your heart.

Then, with a feeling of self-worth and value, look at what you've wanted to do for a while. It will often be different from what your brain has been conditioned to think. It might even feel "alien" to state your desire. If it does, that's perfectly OK!

Your true heart knows what north is for you. Don't let yourself pretend you don't. Say this out loud: "My true heart knows north. I've known all along; I might just be scared to see it."

Deep breath.

Does anything in your body get activated when you say that out loud? I usually yawn deeply when I say things like this.

We will work with the heart first, the brain next. For now, let's find out what's within your beautiful heart.

## Working with the big blanket desire, before we move to the financial desires...

Step 1 – Place a hand on your heart, so it knows you are there with it.

Step 2 – Breath in a sense of value into your heart.

Step 3 – Say: "Hello, heart that I love, what is it you desire with all your being?"

You'll notice that it feels really darn good to do this. And the answers will be shockingly simple.

"To be happy."

"To be content."

"To create something meaningful."

The heart likes to speak in simple language. These answers are life changing if you listen and follow them.

What comes up for you? What was your first answer?

**My friends had these answers...**

"To create, to create, to create."

"To create my own freedom."

"To be fully present with those that I love."

"Endless abundance."

"To assist those who need help."

Gosh, isn't the heart incredible? What wonderful desires.

Now, let's drill even deeper into the same question and add a specific context around this blanket desire.

Step 1 – Place a hand on your heart so it knows you are there with it.

Step 2 – Breathe a sense of value into your heart.

Step 3 – Say: "Hello, heart that I love. What is it you desire in regards to finances?"

My answer is, "to provide for my family."

The heart does not need to justify this answer. Let it be. Whatever your answer is, just let it be. You don't need to explain yourself to anyone, not even yourself.

**My friends said...**

"First-class living."

"Rich, at least to not have to work."

"More than I know how to spend."

"To give freely without worry."

"To not worry about finances."

Whatever your desire is right now, honor it like a best friend. If you feel vulnerable when you say it, that is really good. If it is hard to say, I understand.

For me, I use this desire "to provide for my family" as an example because providing for my family is the thing I feel really scared of because it goes deeper than money.

Business was less scary than family.

If I failed at business, it wouldn't hurt as much as if I failed at family, so I chose business first to build stronger self-esteem, so I could later pursue family. I also did it to give myself income so I could be certain I'd be able to take care of a family.

What do you do if you don't hear anything when you ask?

You might not be able to hear the truth of what your heart has to say. You might not have listened to your heart in a long time. It might take a while to reconnect with the voice of your heart. I'd encourage you to keep an open mind and wait until your heart is ready to be heard.

You can put your hand on your heart and breath in a sense of value over and over again until it's ready to be heard.

### "What if I don't come up with a desire?"

The greatest gift you could ever receive is the gift of your heart. The most precious relationship you will ever have is with the one with your own heart.

You must become internally directed to find that endless source of strength and power. The external world will not care about you as much as you do. Go internal. Keep asking until you know, it will come.

# CHAPTER 5:

# FINDING CONFIDENCE

There is a quick route to finding confidence.

Confidence can quickly come when you know who you are, and what's important to you.

And when you are comfortable being honest about it.

The next step is now to uncover a powerful realization about yourself to keep you motivated. With motivation and confidence, you've got some serious power under the hood. To do that, we want to discover the conscious and unconscious motivations we carry around with your hearts declaration.

● Related to motivation, let me briefly talk about proving yourself. If you're doing something to prove yourself, you will likely lose motivation often because it's not a heart based desire.

Deep down past all the conditioning, the heart already knows it's worth is beyond words.

If you are stuck looking for approval, and if following a real desire brings up a lot for you, consider you may be worried you are not enough. That's simply a lie. You are.

It is in fact safe to follow your real desires.

You will better find more lasting motivation when you are happy, serving others, and making others happy. But be honest with yourself. Be where you are. You can be selfish here. Because now that we've got your heart's declaration, we are going to root it down into your core so deep that you become wildly congruent.

To do this, we are going to use a "What's Most Important?" framework to uncover hidden motivations. Credit for this framework goes to Eben Pagan and Joe Stumpf.

Both great dudes.

With this framework, you repeat the question "What's most important?" until you've dug all the way down to the root. Usually, you'll need to ask the question five to seven times.

Make sure to use the word "what" instead of "why."
"What" uncovers motivation.
"Why" uncovers justification.

Motivation helps with action, so let's find that by asking the "what" question. Once we uncover the conscious and (hidden) unconscious motivations for something, we have greater freedom to pursue it.

Our conscious motivations are usually general and simple but don't hold enough juice for us to take action on. Things like, "Oh, I want freedom," "I don't want a boss," or "I'm tired of being poor."

● Unconscious motivations are sneaky, they can be healing and regenerative or destructive. They can be things like... "I want every human to feel like I'm the most powerful person alive! Then no one will ever doubt me, hurt me, or not love me! I must be loved. I must protect myself."

This is ultimately not a healing motivation to be driven from. You want to heal this.

Once you see these motivations clearly, you are free from the compulsion driving you. <u>Being driven by compulsions is not healthy</u>. When you are free, you have a greater sense of ease to pursue your desires and will become even more successful (without these things controlling you).

To get started, you'll ask yourself...What's most important to me about [insert dream-desire of the heart]?

Then you'll follow up each question with a little variation so it works for you.

This can get real really fast. Let me show you what happened with my desire to provide for my family.

## Using The What's Most Important Framework On Myself

**Dane, what's most important to you about providing for your family?**
I get to love another being that is my own.
(Oh, that's nice. I didn't know that was there! Let's continue.)

**What's most important to you about having the chance to love another being that is your own?**
It feels like it is why I am here.

**What's most important to you about that?**
Loving is all I want to do. (Started to get dizzy here.)

**What's most important to you about loving is all I want to do?**
I often get lost proving things instead of loving others.

**What's most important to you not getting lost and instead loving others?**
I really want to be with people. Like really be with them. Not just think I am. But being with them, with a relaxed heart.

**What's most important to you about being with someone with a relaxed heart?**
It's where my heart likes to sing.

**What's most important to you about being where your heart likes to sing?**
So someone else can see my true heart.

**What's most important to you about someone seeing your true heart?**
Then I will no longer be lonely.

**What's most important to you about no longer being lonely?**
Then I can be with my family again, once I feel my heart has been seen.

I asked the question nine times, and it rocked me! I discovered I don't want to be lonely. This is huge to be clear on. This discovery also allowed me to heal my loneliness by seeing my own heart. That's what I really wanted... to know and see my own heart... even more than someone else seeing it.

This is a wonderful process. I'm sure your insights will be wonderful too. And remember, yours can be anything!

One of my friends said the true desire of his heart was "to create, to create, to create." Then when he asked, "What's most important?" he was in tears when he realized his deepest motivation was to create to touch hearts, to keep a family together, so no one ever had to leave.

He just happened to be adopted. He let out some major sobs, released very old trauma, and experienced a new understanding around his heart's true desire "to create, to create, to create."

That's powerful stuff.

Another one of my friend's desires was "to assist those who need help." When we asked, "What's most important?" he became deeply connected to the idea that everyone deserves a second chance.

Can you imagine the motivation this can create? It is way beyond status, money, and success. It's about unconditional love. It would be hard to give up on a task with this knowledge of ourselves.

No matter if you want status, fame, money, freedom, or to love the world with all your heart and give others a second chance...as long as you are clear, and you are motivated, and it is your vision, and it's made in love for you, it is perfectly OK.

## ● What to do if shame comes up around your desire.

Try this process for 30 seconds as an experiment...

1.  Make sure you are in a quiet place.
2.  Put your hand on your heart.
3.  Take a deep breath.
4.  Say out loud, "I feel this shame as totally real and not really who I am deep down."
5.  Let out any sounds or movements necessary until you feel complete.

It can be wild to realize we hold shame around a desire. Give yourself all the space you need to be with it. Shame is best met as a good friend you haven't seen in a long time. Love it without believing it is who you are. You will eventually be liberated.

Your heart Is a tender muscle, and it loves when you place your hand over it. Do it often.
OK.
To recap, you've got the dream-desire of your heart.
You've got your core motivation.
Both the initial motivation and the deep-down hidden one.
But alas, self-sabotage is real. Taking action is difficult at times.
So let us address that next.

# CHAPTER 6:

# FACE YOUR MIND

Years ago, I was on a call with a gentleman who had a bad business idea. It wasn't solid, *but he liked it.* Like a house of cards, the slightest wind could blow it over. He could not see it was a bad idea because something in him was holding on strong.

His grip blinded him.

What made it even trickier was his potential customers said they liked the idea, but did not want to pay for it.

> "Yeah, I like this idea!"
> "Would you buy it?"
> "Uhmmmm, talk to me when it's complete."

Oh, this is a big red flag.

This can be a devilish situation to get caught in. Being so close to a winning business made this man "hold on for dear life."

I asked the gentleman if he could just drop the idea and find another. His face turned deep red. I slowed down and allowed him to experience the question. I thought to myself, *this probably isn't gonna go well.*

After a bit, I asked, "What's going on? Are you okay?"

He got even more angry.
> "This has to work. It has to!" he said.

I paused for a moment. I felt sadness in my heart. I asked, "Do you know what has you saying that?"

"I just really want *something* to work. Really bad!"

Then I froze. I didn't have the training yet to facilitate such a situation at the time.

His tight grip totally screwed him, as it does to us all.

So what compels someone to hold on to a bad idea? Here is my hypothesis.

He thinks he's close to success. He's gotta hold on. He thinks it'll only happen one time. He doesn't believe he could ever do it again. He feels deeply inadequate and that he must get lucky.

So he believes he only has one chance to be successful.

And this little belief will keep a person in a bad business, an incompatible relationship, or a crappy job. Try saying it outloud and see if it rings true. "I only have one chance to be successful."

Give yourself a little love if you feel that one. We can clear it later.

I think this man was driven by a deep belief that he was unworthy and that he had to prove otherwise. He had a safe income from a job, a stable life. He just wanted this new business to work so badly it made his face red when it was at risk.

This isn't a *bug* for us. This is a *feature* most of us share.
Guess what happened? He burned out and quit.

When you're free from these compulsions, you can see clearly. When you can see clearly, success is one objective decision after another, instead of a game of luck or chance.

Burning out and quitting is self-sabotage in action. So, let's get clear. What is self-sabotage? Self-sabotage is our unconscious beliefs making themselves a reality.

From my experience, I've seen that there are two issues that will sabotage you. The first is the beliefs you hold. The second is the identity—"who" you think you are... the person behind all of the beliefs.

These are the two issues we need to look at. And it's a tricky business. Often false beliefs and the identity you hold will appear together. For example, you might think: *Business is risky, and I'll lose everything* (belief), *which will cause people to see me as a worthless failure* (identity).

This sentence can manipulate all of your behavior from the shadows. Even if you know deep down it isn't true.

We must learn to focus the intellect in a different way to transcend these beliefs. Our instincts are to fix, change, or cover up these thoughts. Unfortunately, those actions just reinforce beliefs and keep them in place. Instead, we want to fully love these beliefs until they no longer hold the same influence.

We love them, but we do not believe them. Just like we would love and hold a hysterical child but not buy into their drama.

Let's do that now.

We will be taking two steps here. We will transform a thought on the root level, and then we will transcend the belief system altogether.

Before we begin, I want to give proper credit and a big thanks to my mindset mentor Brian Adler. His work is infused into the following pages, and I recommend you learn all you can from this wonderful man. If you'd like more on this, you can find details on Brian's mindset course at StartFromZero.com/Yes.

And you can try our wonderful process to unblock yourself for free at StartFromZero.com/Yes.

## ◉ Step 1: Discover & Uncover

Now, we need to find out what kind of thoughts you are holding about your big desires. If these thoughts are limiting, you'll want to address them gently but head-on. Remember, beliefs don't make rational sense. It's important to honor the irrationality of them.

My dream desire was to provide for my family. So, I'm going to ask what I believe about that.

In this step you ask yourself, "Do I believe anything negative about [insert key desire of your heart right now]?"

In other words, you might be asking yourself, "Do I believe anything negative about...

> "My desire to provide for my family?"
> "My desire to have a business?"
> "My desire to sing?"
> "My desire for music?"
> "My desire for good sex?"
> "My desire to protect and provide for my family?"
> "My desire to assist those in need?"
> "My desire to create, create, create?"

You want to ask this about anything you are struggling to take action on.

Here's how the process went for me:

**Do I believe anything negative about providing for my family?**

I'll never be able to do it. I'll fail.

Yikes. Let's work with this discovery now.

## Step 2: Transform One At A Time

First, we are going back to Byron Katie's five-step process called *The Work*. *The Work* consists of four questions and a turnaround statement. In this case, I am adding a sixth step to her process to include a step from my mindset mentor Brian Adler.

Brian Adler has the most effective process for mindset transformation I have yet to see, which is why I created a course with him.

To provide you with the most effective process for this book, I'm combining these two processes.

Hey, if it works, it works.

| Bryon Katie's Process | Process With Additional Step 6 |
|---|---|
| 1. Is that belief true? | 1. Is that belief true? |
| 2. Can you absolutely know it's true? | 2. Can you absolutely know it's true? |
| 3. How do you react? What happens when you believe that thought? | 3. How do you react? What happens when you believe that thought? |
| 4. Who would you be without that thought? | 4. Who would you be without that thought? |
| 5. Turn the thought around. Is the opposite true or truer than the original thought? | 5. Turn the thought around. Is the opposite true or truer than the original thought? |
| | 6. Now go back and *notice* instead of believing both thoughts. |

The reason we are modifying and adding a step is because we don't want to get caught trying to improve or change a belief; we want to wake up from the entire sense of a belief altogether.

"Notice versus believe" is the way to do that. In the ideal scenario we are not bound to any beliefs about a topic at all. Being in the mystery, being without a concrete opinion, is infinite freedom. In this state, everything is an experiment. (This is worth contemplating.)

Keep the good beliefs you love. For example, "family is awesome." Or "friends are cool." But sometimes family *isn't* awesome. And sometimes friends *aren't* cool. It's especially important to notice instead of believe when these situations are present.

The bottom line is that you can use beliefs that work for you. If it gets you taking action and you are happy, more power to you. I recommend just waking up from belief systems altogether.

Now it's time for the experiment. I'm going to show you the process with the belief that "tilted" my head the most. This belief really puzzled me when it came through.

> Belief: I'll fail to provide for my family.
>
> Yeah, this one really stops me from living presently with my family.
>
> Let's begin.
>
> **Is that belief true?** Well, yes! Duh! (My head nods big).
>
> **Can you absolutely know that it's true?** Hmm... I cannot.
>
> **How do you react, what happens, when you believe that thought?**
>
> I feel really sad. Really collapsed. I want to hide out of shame and embarrassment. I even refuse good things from happening on an unconscious level. A lot of shame.

It's like pure shame. Right in the center of my solar plexus. With this feeling I can't imagine anyone loving me. I even see myself leaving family, leaving friends, leaving relationships. This feeling is really subtle but very convincing.

It parades around in all kinds of thoughts and circumstances but it's really just one thing.

Shame.

**Who would you be without that thought?**

Without the thought of I'll be a failure and the shame involved? Without those thoughts, I'd be free. I'd love more.

**Turn the thought around.**

I've never failed to provide for my family.

Dang, this is wild. That's totally true. I never have.

So now that we've updated belief, now it's time to take it a level deeper and exit the belief system altogether.

*Belief*: I'll fail to provide for my family.

*Now notice instead of believe*: I start to gain a deeper perspective while doing this. What does that belief even mean? It does not have a hold on me. It seems like a really solid lie. Like it is almost a thought used to hurt myself.

Let's now exit the flipped positive belief.

*Belief*: I've never failed to provide for my family.

*Now notice instead of believe*: I see that while it's true, it's also just a belief. What's more important than this belief is how I show up in each moment.

So now you can see that there is an epic freedom in transforming *and then* transcending the belief system altogether. We transform by reversing and transcend by noticing instead of believing. It can start to make thoughts and beliefs feel like a game we've been playing this whole time.

And hopefully, it opens up a great sense of humor and release for you.

Now I want to show you another belief I've cleared before in regards to something very different from business, but it's related. Singing. Learning to sing has helped a lot with self acceptance. A lot. Singing is very healing for me to do. It brings me into my body. So it was an expression I wanted to get deeper with.

Let's get into it.

*Belief*: My ugly heart shows when I sing. (Daggers, whoa.)

Remember, these beliefs are often irrational and in the unconscious; it's important to be honest with ourselves. And that is what was honestly there for me.

Deep breath. Let's begin.

**Is that belief true?**

Very true!

**Can I absolutely know that it's true?**

I guess not. People seem to be happy when I sing.

**How do I react, what happens, when I believe that thought?**

I stop singing. Dead in my tracks. When people compliment my voice, it doesn't make sense, so I shut down.

**Who would I be without that thought?**

I'd be free, and my tender heart would feel more playful.

**Now turn that thought around.**

When I sing, people get the chance to feel my heart and soul, and it moves them.

**Now notice instead of believing both thoughts.**

*Negative Belief:* My ugly heart shows when I sing.

*Notice Instead of believe:* Haha, this is just weird. It is almost like self abuse to think that way. No. It is. No one is thinking I have an ugly heart. And if someone is, they are crazy.

*Positive Belief:* When I sing, people get the chance to feel my heart and soul, and it moves them.

*Notice instead of believe:* I notice there's an even bigger game at play. Bigger than what I believe. To me, singing feels like an expression that gets recorded in the halls of time for all of time. Singing feels like a cosmic expression that goes beyond space. Singing is how you hang out with the divine realm.

Singing is starting to seem like an even better idea for me.

Now a note about these examples: both of the beliefs I worked with evoked a strong sense of identity.

● *Identity.*
Identity is a story of who we think we are,

Identity is the second of the two things that can stop us, and it can be very tricky to deal with. These identities hold on for dear life, and the best way to shift is to love the identity exactly as it is. Don't believe it; just fully love and honor it. It can be a tricky thing to do when we've been at war with ourselves for so long.

You've seen people try to ignore their inner voices only to get beaten down and quit, right? This is identity, and it needs gentle compassion. Identities are real, but they are not truly who we are.

Identities can shift over time. So then how can they actually be true?

How do you shift an identity? Like I said, by loving it because you know it isn't really true. You can fully love it as much as it needs when you realize it really isn't who you are.

Deep breath.

Freedom is here for us all. Compassion for ourselves is the only way.

> **My examples**
> Dream desire: To provide for my family.
> Negative belief: I will fail to provide for my family.
> Turned-around belief: I have never failed to provide for my family.

> **My examples**
> Dream desire: To sing to get out of my head.
> Negative belief: My ugly heart shows when I sing.
> Turned-around belief: People are moved when they see my heart from singing.

> **Let's look at my female friend's examples.**
> Dream desire: To be a wealthy, successful entrepreneur.
> Negative belief: I let myself get pushed around to make it happen.
> Turned-around belief: I am strong and powerful, and I create from strength.

> **Or how about another woman's.**
> Dream desire: Freedom.

Negative belief: It's hard and almost impossible to achieve.

Turned-around belief: It is in fact achievable.

**One more example from a father.**

Dream desire: To provide control and security for my family.

Negative belief: No one in my family has done it.

Turned-around belief: No one in my family has done it, yet.

## The Steps To Transform

1. Take your key desire and ask about the hidden negative beliefs you hold.

2. Put them into Byron Katie's process called "The Work."

3. Use her five-question process for one belief at a time.

4. Once the thought is transformed, use the "notice vs. believe" to exit both beliefs.

5. Enjoy having your foot off the brake.

What's in the way *is* the way. What's in the way is a friend that needs your love. What's in the way is your doorway to freedom.

OK...

So, now you've gotten clear on the map for getting yourself across the desert. You've got a declaration. You've got the tools to deal with inner conflicts of belief and identity, which I just showed you. We've got the car, and the gas tank is full, and we've gotten our foot off the brake.

We are ready to drive.

*Disclaimer:* Being hard on yourself, critical of yourself, and hateful of yourself will simply not work.

There is a little known feeling that can free you no matter what you are going through if you get lucky enough to feel it. It's such a powerful feeling that it can unlock your stuckness, shut down your own judgements so you are kind to yourself, and allow you the space to be exactly as you are.

It's the root of self-acceptance and unconditional love, which makes you unstoppable.

Now, this feeling is important to find because this process can be very threatening to do.

Very. Threatening.

Every single response your body has is OK.

Every difficulty you have is OK. Even what doesn't feel OK is still OK.

If something is difficult, it doesn't say anything about who you are. We all have difficulties.

Your shoulders might rise. Your heart might beat faster. You might not be able to see straight. You might want to put this book down. If you feel threatened by doing any of this work, please allow yourself the space for that feeling. It is real. Your body is tense for a good, compassionate reason; it's likely trying to protect you out of love, and there is wisdom there.

Love for yourself is so powerful to realize, recognize, and feel. Love everything that comes up. Even the difficulty. Even if the emotion feels like it's stopping you. Love that. If you get angry at loving the feeling that's stopping you, love the anger. Keep loving the experiences until you open up to the truth.

That nothing can actually stop you. You only believe it can.

So what's that little-known feeling?

Compassion for the hardest thing. Making friends with the worst aspect of your mind.

But don't force it. You will find it naturally through loving each response that comes up. Love everything that comes up. Please allow yourself to uncover compassion towards every response you have, but don't force it. Let it come about naturally.

Once you fully and directly see what is causing struggle, compassion will automatically unlock. It is truly the fastest and best way to free yourself. And it's honestly the only way I found that really works.

We have a free process that teaches this for free at StartFromZero.com/Yes.

Now you have the dream desire of your heart, and you are taking off the weights from the negative beliefs, you are ready to walk freely.

Let's talk about aligning your being...and where to drive...this next step is huge!

# CHAPTER 7:

# ALIGN YOUR ENVIRONMENT

Next, we align your environment in four key areas by accepting that we are faulty at times without proper support.

Have you ever heard someone say... "Oh, I'm not a name person, I forget names," and they do nothing about it?

They go on forgetting names because they don't really care, which is actually the truth. If they truly cared to remember, they would.

But what about this... Have you ever met someone who carried a notebook around to write a name down when they met someone?

There was such a fellow.
He wrote down your name when he met you.

You ask, "What are you doing?"
He says, "Oh, I have trouble with names, so I like to write them down."

This experience is so rare to see. And then again, so is extreme success. This man went on to become a president. Mr. Bill Clinton.

Would you have voted for him if you had the pleasure of watching him write your name down? That would certainly make me feel important. And I've heard Bill Clinton has a way of making you feel like the only person in the world when you're talking with him. What a charmer, if you know what I mean.

So why am I telling you this? The point of that story is that the brain is faulty at times and needs help. We need a structure that helps us to fly like Bill had with his notebook.

So I've got one. This structure includes four areas: Thoughts, Emotions, Environment, and Schedule. We are looking for one big idea in each area.

Ask yourself...

1. What primary thought can I hold to pursue my dream of X?
2. What primary feeling can I insert to pursue my dream of X?
3. What primary change can I make to my environment to pursue X?
4. What primary change can I make to my schedule to pursue X?

Let me show you how those four questions worked for my dream.

**What primary thought can I hold to pursue my dream to provide for my family?**
Thought: That I matter to my family.

**What primary feeling can I cultivate to pursue my dream to provide for my family?**
Emotion: I am a provider.

**How can I set up or change my environment to make my dream to provide for my family possible?**
Environment: Wake up in gratitude and prayer for the family in my life and give them kisses.

**How can I set up my schedule first thing in the morning to support my dream to provide for my family?**
Schedule: Pray over each member of the family that they are safe loved and cared for.

Remember. These ideas need to be simple. We want our living circumstances to aid us, not destroy us.

Now imagine the amount of self-love you will feel when you've taken these four steps? Let me know what you end up coming up with at StartFromZero.com/Yes.

Here's an example from a fellow entrepreneur.

> **Thought:** I am a humble entrepreneur. I love making profits so I can solve more problems and help more people.
> **Feeling:** I am already taken care of.
> **Environment:** I'm hanging out with the right crowd so the right people will show up.
> **Schedule:** In bed at 8:30 p.m.

Here's another example:

> **Thought:** I can have financial and time freedom.
> **Feeling:** Joy.
> **Environment:** I can put my computer on the dining room table so I can work on my business after everyone goes to bed or first thing in the morning.
> **Schedule:** I can go online and provide one solution to one business right away in the morning just for the practice of serving.

Here's another example:

> **Thought:** I can create time to give others my full attention while working on my dream.
> **Feeling:** Calm and surrendered.
> **Environment:** Free of big distractions (nothing but the work item in front of me).
> **Schedule:** Use the morning to plan my day and make sure my work time is for work and my family time is family.

Now, these steps are simple but profound. If your commitment is to live this, you will transform.

Building the muscle of discipline and consistency will render you unstoppable.

Here is where we are now. We have...

* The dream desire.
* The most important motivation.
* The negative beliefs discovered.
* The beliefs transcended.
* The aligned life.

Let's wrap it all up nicely with a prescription for your heart...

## Prescribe: Create a Physical Reminder, Such as a Business Card, and Put the Reminder All Over Your Home

Next, I went to Moo at StartFromZero.com/Moo and made cards, put them in my wallet, on my desk, and around my house. I breathe them in whenever I can to reprogram my state of mind and brain.

I made these awesome, super thick business cards (an order of 50), created specifically from what I discovered using this process!

This is the front:
Those words are very healing to breathe into my sense of identity.

I matter to my family
*I have never failed my family*
*I move people when I sing*
*I give thanks for each family member in the morning*

This is the back:

So now you have a custom prescription for your own heart. If you really breath your own words in, you'll be giving yourself life. These are very different than affirmations. This is a custom prescription. Words give life.

Especially when they come from within you.

I love Moo, get your cards made at StartFromZero.com/Moo (affiliate link, I do get compensated, so thank you in advance if you do purchase from this link.)

# CHAPTER 8:

# DEALING WITH LOSING MOTIVATION

Let's discuss the real reason why it's so easy to give up and why it's so hard to change.

It is commonly known that we lose motivation if things don't work. But what's less known is that even when things are working, we still lose motivation.

In both circumstances, it is still the result of the same thing.

I had a friend who struggled with her weight for years. She had started and stopped working out over and over and over again.

One day she decided to make a real change and started to work out again. This time she was really committed. But this time as she started making real progress and got in shape, she started showing off her bikini body at the beach, and she started losing motivation.

That's right.

As she started succeeding and seeing results... she started to topple... just as things were getting good.

I see this same thing happen to myself and others who start a business and then stop.

My friend was so frustrated, she told me, "I just can't get myself to do what I want!"

Here is what was going on.

What happened is she started changing externally, but the internal identity of "I'm fat," started making a bunch of noise against her.

This is because she didn't first work with the deeper identity that said: "I'm a fat person."

Identity can be extremely difficult to work with without proper guidance. And even with guidance it can be very very hard. I've actually given up on goals before because of how difficult it was to shift an identity.

I thought to myself, "if it's this difficult, there's no way this can be right, I better give up."

Until I realized how much greater I am than any identity I hold.

Identity is debilitating without the proper guidance. But here's the good news about identity.

## Identity is only a thought.

Identity is truly just a thought that, once noticed and held with love, can lose it's hypnotic trance on you.

Where most people go wrong is they think they need to fix or get rid of or change an identity. Many programs online successfully sell you this.

"Fix your identity! Change it in days!" They will say.

But if you go out and try to fix or change your identity, it will actually reinforce that it is a problem and keep it there.

## Here's what you need to do.

My mindset mentor Brian Adler reminds us, "Our identities don't want us to believe them; they just want us to listen to them like a friend while holding them with love as real but not true."

Real.

But not true.

Identity is who you think you are, on a deep, unconscious level. But it's not truly who you are. Unconscious means you can't really see it; you just watch yourself living out the behavior. And the most freeing thing I could ever tell you about identity comes from Brian.

> "When it comes to identity, our goal is to hold these things as real, but not true. Because it is definitely real you feel this way, but it is not who you are. That means we can hold these identities like you would a crying baby, until it stops making noise. Then you are free to work out or do whatever it is you want to do."

Have you ever wondered why you don't do what you say? Old identities cry out, "come back! This is what we know!" they tell you. Resistance comes in.

## Identity isn't personal, it's just acting out what it believes, and this can shift!

So first, please recognize any of the judgment you might have. We all struggle at times. In many cases lack of motivation comes down to an issue with a belief or an identity.

I spoke with another person who had the greatest difficulties making money until she used our DJP framework to discover she had a hidden identity of "I'm a poor person."

Once she discovered that, she cried for hours and began shifting it, just by seeing it directly.

Now making money is starting to become easier.

## Here are a couple of questions you can ask to troubleshoot your motivation.

* Is there a belief I'm holding right now that's causing me to lose motivation?
* Is there an identity or story I'm holding about myself that's causing me to lose motivation?
* Am I just being lazy?

❶ Cultivate the muscle of taking action through resistance. Hold the resistance at the same time you act. It'll feel like you're drowning above water, but eventually you'll be swimming.

❷ Move slow. Act. Love. It'll transform with hard work.

And it does take hard work.

One of the biggest things to watch out for is cutting off parts of yourself to succeed or move forward. You want to bring every part of you into this new world you're creating. Don't fragment yourself.

If you apply this process of belief transformation and holding identities with compassion when they arise, you'll increase your motivation and strengthen your confidence and self-esteem.

And if you ever need help, please try our free process at StartFromZero.com/Yes.

> **Here is an example of the embodied process I do in real-time when I'm stuck.**
>
> *I'm having trouble writing this section. It's extremely difficult. I reread sentences that I just wrote and see all kinds of typos. Whoa. I can't even see what I'm writing.*
>
> I hear what I want to say in my mind, but when I refer back to the sentence, it is not what I thought I wrote. What the heck is this

sentence? Did I write this?

I sit back and allow space for these feelings.

*Oh, I'm disoriented.*

*I can't see what I'm writing.* Immediately I feel my chest. It aches. I cough. I want to perform really well and do a good job for you, the reader, I honor that desire. It's vulnerable. My hands start to tingle. I'm starting to feel excited. *What's going on with all this?* I ask.

*You're freeing yourself from a lot of fear, and that is terrifying.* Ah, that's nice to hear. But I'm still judging my experience right now. I don't want anyone to know I'm terrified of losing fear, it's kept me safe. I start to feel a sound of pain that wants to come from my chest. I make the crying sound. This sound scares me. My face winces. My left eye closes. *Gosh, writing leaves me so vulnerable.* I tense up to protect my body, expecting an attack. My bullies from the past flood my mind. My shoulders rise. My eyes get blurry. I want this pain to go away. I let myself feel numb.

I take a breather.

I hang out with that new felt insight. *Writing is so vulnerable. I guess I have a difficult relationship with vulnerability.*

A new desire emerges: *Gosh, I really hope I do a good job. Wow. I want to do a good job.* I honor this desire of wanting to do a good job. Like a long lost friend, I befriend it. I really want to do a good job. This motivation was in the background until now. It opens me up to feel. I keep saying it to hang out with it.

*I really want to do a good job.*

I allow that to wash over me. Then I start to see where I struggle. I befriend the sense of struggle. I befriend the sense of difficulty.

Usually when things are difficult, I try to engage my mind to fix the feeling. Now I just embrace the simple feeling of "difficult."

A new sentence emerges: *This book is a big deal to me.*

My head starts to nod. Dang. It is. I've been playing it down like it isn't. But it is a big deal to me. I feel my legs flush with a bunch of energy that feels very light.

I befriend and allow that sentence to be felt. *Whoa. I never really let myself feel this.*

*This book is a big deal to me. Can I let something be a big deal to me?* I really struggle with this.

Honoring this sentence is incredibly moving. But I'm afraid of feeling attacked for letting something be a big deal to me. My bullies reemerge in my mind.

This is important to me, and I'm afraid of being attacked.

*I'm afraid of others attacking me.* I place my attention on this. The fear of attack is crippling. I feel like I'm 12. I clear my throat and honor and allow this awareness. I sense no feeling of safety. This cripples my brain for sure.

Then I pull the Jedi move. I ask, *Who is the identity of the person who is having all of these experiences?*

Someone who is afraid.

I cry.

And then, I move to holding the identity behind all of this experience. I hold and honor this sense of an identity as real but not true. I notice instead of believe.

I taste metal in my mouth. I feel fists hitting me and my head getting smashed into the ground. Memories of those who were in pain causing me pain. I love them for what they taught me, that pain causes pain.

But it's ok now, because love causes love.

It's difficult. I could probably use another therapy session on this. I'll get some help.

But freedom starts to come in. I'm starting to feel lighter after being so honest with myself.

Now... I'm ready to write the book and continue to let the feelings come.

And that is how I allow energies and find identities.

To wrap up, here are the rules:

1. Honor everything that comes up.
2. Let everything be real but not true to who you are. Really honor it as real.
3. Notice instead of believing everything to gain perspective.
4. Keep going until you feel the space open up.

In closing, this can be very difficult and many times it helps to have training and facilitation. We have a free process that helps you do this at http://StartFromZero.com/Yes.

In the next section, I'll show you how to ask for help and what I do when I need help.

# CHAPTER 9:

# LIBERATE YOUR SOUL BY ASKING FOR HELP

## How does one liberate their own potential?

There's a lot of hype and confusion around what liberating your potential really means, so I'll make this short and clear.

Liberating your potential is about following your soul's voice with unwavering faith.

So here's what you do:

Love your ego as it is, with all it's voices, and let your soul's voice guide you. You'll become a pioneer at your craft and do remarkable things.

This entire transformation section you read previously was about waking up your soul's voice and reprogramming the mind to honor and follow it.

But you will likely need help. Let me show you how to ask for help when you need it.

## How to Ask for Help Powerfully...

Let's make it really easy for you to ask for help from a place of power. I highly recommend you work with at least one coach you trust. I have listed my favorite coach at the bottom of this chapter. This coach understands how to help you make the deep identity shifts required to succeed. I asked them for guidance many times while writing this book.

Developing this book was hard.

It's OK to do what is hard. Remember that.

It's tricky to pick an effective coach who knows what they are doing, which is why I've included a recommendation below. But you can use anyone you want. You'll need someone who can help with belief shifts and identity transformation.

Not someone who will force you to achieve a goal.

Find a coach who's process is rooted in compassion; that'll take you further. I recommend you do 12 weeks of coaching at a time, focusing on your biggest issue.

Here is the email you can send to a life coach. It will blow them away.

> Subject: Could you help me?
>
> Hello [insert name],
>
> I found you online, and you seem like the kind of person who could help me. I'm looking for someone who can help me with the deeper issues that come up when pursuing a meaningful dream.
>
> I get stuck in my head.
>
> I've just recently made a declaration to [insert declaration], but it's very scary for me, and I need some help with the fears, beliefs, and emotions that come up.
>
> I've done some deeper motivation reflection and found out my core motivation for [insert declaration] is to [insert deepest found motivation].

I have aligned my life in four core areas. My thoughts, feelings, environment, and schedule are all aligned to support this desire I have.

But I know I will encounter deeper identity-level issues that are going to make it really hard at times. I know I'm human and will need help.

That's why I'm looking for a weekly coach to help me stay accountable and help me process the emotions, limiting beliefs, and identities that come up along the way. I'd like to work with you for 12 weeks to see if we could transform my blocks in that period of time.

Would you be available for a chat?

*[Your name]*

Now, if you send that email to a life coach, you will be a breath of fresh air to them. I can picture a life coach reading this email and thinking, *Holy crap! I'd love to have a client like this.* Just make sure you work with someone who is experienced. As I've said, ideally, you'll want to work with a coach weekly for 12 weeks. Spend no less than $1,500 (too cheap) and no more than $6,000 (too much) for the three-month period.

Will the money spent be worth it? The ROI on coaching and therapy is higher than any dollar I've ever spent. Remember that. I have spent as much as 50% of my income on courses, coaches, programs, etc., and it's been the best money I've spent. Don't be cheap. Invest in yourself. People do know some sweet stuff, and it's usually hidden away in courses.

May I ask you something?

Will you allow yourself to want something with all of your heart?

Go forward with love for all of life.

Once you feel ready, let's move forward to building the four entrepreneurial brains!

## ●Taking Action: You've Got Four Things to Do. Do Them Quickly to Plant the Seeds... So They Can Grow.

**Follow This Process by Yourself for Just Two Full Hours & See What Happens.**

This might seem like a lot of hard work. But it's really only two hours. Set aside a timer with two full hours and complete all of the steps in this section.

- 1. Make your heart's declaration.
- 2. Resolve the inner conflicts.
- 3. Align your life in the four areas.
- 4. Create your custom prescription.

Then once you've done that, share it in our community here: http://StartFromZero.com/Yes.

Have fun finding out more about yourself.

Note: It's also OK to just do one item at a time. Give yourself a week to go through it slowly. You can just do one item one day at a time. Make your heart's declaration one day. Do the motivations another day. Resolve the inner conflicts another day. Etc...

Now let's get to the four brains. They are awesome.

## End The War With Your Mind To Follow Your Soul's Voice By Using My Favorite Coach

The quickest way to end the war with your mind is to find the very worst thing within your mind, and make friends with it.

This can be challenging. But extremely rewarding.

For 1 on 1 help with this very thing, I recommend hiring Brian Adler for 12 week sprints at his website MakeFriendsWithTheMind.com

For more affordable group help to Make Friends With Your Own Mind, I recommend StartFromZero.com/Yes

# THE ONE DAY EXPERIMENT:
# ALIGNING YOUR HEART'S DESIRES

Try this for one morning. If you like it keep going for another.

The thing you love the most might be the hardest thing to do.

Here you'll see compassion is truly medicine for epic, relaxed achievement. Even if you're angry. Find compassion for the anger. Anger can be intelligent.

Remember the resistance can be a good thing.

For example, on just another average morning, here's what can happen when I'm starting a routine that's important to me. The alarm rings. I groan. I go to meditate on gratitude and my body starts twisting inside. *Can I meditate this morning? Can I?! It's just for 30 minutes?*

This stuff is for real. I believe the greatest challenge you will overcome is your own resistance.

Let's see what happens for you.

1. Write down the chief desire of your heart.

2. Write down the positive new beliefs you have created.

3. After your morning routine, schedule your first 30 minutes to focus on your chief desire.

# THE FOUR BUILDABLE BRAINS

People often ask, "how long does this take, and what is required?"

To that I say, "when it works, it works. Zero months to two years depending on how committed you are."

For Andrea, she was fast. She was only five questions and one two-hour presentation away from owning a money-making business. You'll hear about her in the next chapter.

But first, let's get a few things down.

Success is *definitely not* about being right.

It is about surrendering to what works.

"No! It has to be my way! This is the product I want to do! It's about what I want!" says the broke, dumb, idiotic fool.
Yeah, OK. Have fun with that perspective.
It rarely works.

With that said...tactical success when starting from zero comes down to building four brains.

You might be wondering how fast you can get to success. It took me 4 years. My top students "get it" in a single sitting, but to become a way of life, it takes around 2 years.

Bottom line is that this is the fastest path I know of to set yourself and family up safely for a lifetime.

It may seem difficult to you now, that you can start on your own successfully.

No idea?
No experience?
How is that possible?

**This answer might break your brain...**

It is now easier than ever to start and make money. Billionaires and millionaires are made faster than ever in history. It's not getting harder and slower as some would make you believe. It's getting easier and faster.

Warren Buffett became a billionaire at 56 years old. Bill Gates held the record for it as a 31 year old billionaire. Zuckerberg did it by age 23. Kylie Jenner is now the record holder at age 21.

Back in the early 1900's, there were no twenty somethings that were billionaires. It took people like Henry Ford and Rockefeller much more time to hit billionaire status way back then.

This is a remarkable time in history.

*It's getting easier.*
*And faster.*
And...
Right now...
There are many people who need your help.

You'll learn how to help them with this book, even if you don't think you can. If you're 15 years old, you can use this same process. If you live in a foreign country, this process works. If you don't consider yourself intelligent, it still works. The model is elegant and simple.

Starting from zero may seem confusing at the outset, but it's actually the best place to start from. The folks with their own ideas and hidden agendas get eaten alive. You don't need an ego for this to work either. The more humble you are, the better.

I was t-e-r-r-i-f-i-e-d when I was starting out. My brain would shut down, my body would tremor, and my breathing would stop. *Am I making a mistake?!* I'd ask. *No one to depend on but myself?* I'd think. *Figuring out my own health insurance? No benefits? No salary?*

I ran on fear. *If I fail, it's on me. If I got fired from a job, at least I'd have sympathy from others.* Every day I worked on my business, I felt like I was holding my breath, waiting for something to crash.

I felt like a phony. A failure. A fraud. I'd go into hiding for periods out of paralysis. My Xbox was a comforting friend to hide from the fear. I'd look for the simplest products to sell or build because I had no belief in myself. I thought I was getting away with crimes in order to succeed.

The doubt I had was crippling, but somehow I made it out alive. Somehow nothing ever crashed. Fortune favors the bold, they say.

Most of our thoughts lie to us. So who cares what we think? Just do stuff and see what happens.

My hope is that these words comfort you and instill a hope to move forward so you can find your own boldness and courage within. My hope is that in these pages, you can see how remarkable and brilliant and beautiful you can be with the right instruction.

Are you willing to see what might happen if you try?

Let's begin by building the four brains.

# THE SURVEYOR

*The surveyor learns how to see the world in income streams.*

CHAPTER 10:

# THE SURVEYOR

## Learning to See in Income Streams

As a surveyor, you want to teach your brain to see the geographical foundation that every income stream sits on.

This chapter will cover two topics:

1. Examples
2. Business Models

### First, Examples

The fastest way I know to build the surveyor brain is to apply pattern recognition to existing successful businesses using this framework:

Customer. Pain. Solution. Offer.

> Who's the Customer?
> What's the Pain?
> What's the Solution?
> What's the Offer?

Customer. Pain. Solution. Offer.

If you need help remembering C.P.S.O., one of my friends came up with this.

Cats.
Peeing.
Sitting.
Overtly.

Hahaha. He has a twisted imagination... but don't we all?

If you start to think of business in terms of C.P.S.O., you will build a brain that can see in income streams quickly. It'll also help you to avoid getting so dramatic about your own ideas.

Let's use an example of a random business.

*PouPoorri.com* – Spray to stop the odor when you take a dump. I know very little about this business, but I do know that it is extremely successful. *Customer:* Humans embarrassed by the smell of their poo out in a public place or at a friend's home. *Pain:* The humiliation caused by a perfectly normal human action. Poop smells. *Solution:* A spray that covers the top film of the water before you go, so the scent can't escape. *Offer:* $9.95 bottle.

See how this framework allows you to "see" an income stream quickly? You now have the upper hand by using pattern recognition.

Let's look at a more niche income stream:

*BareMetrics.com* – If you own a software company, you need special financial metrics. With this you can plug in your credit card terminal, and this app will read all of your transactions and tell you your critical financial data at a glance. A tool like this is crack for a software owner. Push one button, get financial metrics for your software business. Yum! Last I checked, the owner pulls in over $100,000 per month. *Customer:* Software as a service owners.

**Pain:** Tracking their financial metrics like user drop-off (churn), new sign-ups, monthly recurring revenue, etc.

**Solution:** A one-click integration with a financial dashboard showing all metrics at a glance.

**Offer:** Starting at $50 a month, up to $300 or more.

Let's run one last business through this framework to show you the wide world of business and possibilities.

**GMass.co** – Send mass email campaigns inside of Gmail individually and automatically. This guy was working on another product when he had the problem of sending mass emails. So instead of keeping his other project going, he dropped it and built GMass. GMass makes over $100,000 per month at this time. This product is great because it's not even a stand-alone product. It's just a plugin inside of Gmail. This business deserves our envy. **Customer:** Gmail users who need to send mass emails to 25 addresses or more.

**Pain:** Sending mass emails via bcc or cc with a huge email reply thread sucks.

**Solution:** Mass email six hundred or more at a time in a personalized way.

**Offer:** $6.95 a month to $12.95 a month.

The origin story of GMass.co is more common than you think. He was working on a project no one wanted, but along the way, he built something to help with that project no one wants.

And people want that other thing you built to help yourself. Oh, the hilarity.

Slack was a gaming company that made a chat widget to talk to each other while building their game. They have since dropped the gaming component. They were building something no one wanted (a video game) and along the way, built something (slack) that turned out to be incredibly valuable.

Just to be sure you get this, this is that pattern.

Someone is building widget x to sell, along the way encountered problem y, built widget y to help build widget x.

No one wants widget x.

Everyone wants widget y.

You can see the C.P.S.O. pattern by looking at just a few examples. But if you do this with one hundred businesses, it'll change your brain.

Your brain is probably spinning with what you could build. Go slow. Just keep doing this until you've got a hundred or more examples in your brain. Do it over a couple of weeks. Imagine the business brain you'll build knowing one hundred different income stream examples. You won't be able to believe in scarcity anymore, that's for sure.

Breaking down businesses this way simplifies them to fit into our brain efficiently. There are three big concepts at play here. These concepts are what give you an excellent advantage.

The first is pattern recognition.
The second is applying a framework to organize information.
The third is this actual framework: Customer, Pain, Solution, Offer. CPSO.

If you are impatient to get something working, remember, having a successful business is not what makes you happy. *Being happy is what makes you happy.* Chill out and take your time to find the right business that sets your heart on fire. A rushed business won't work out very well.

⊙ Take your time. Go slow. You want a solid income stream—not a business built on sand.

# ◖ Business Models

You should *obsess* over your business model until it completely takes care of your every need. Do not set up a business placing your customers ahead of you. Create strict requirements for how customers do business with you.

Obsess about what your customers' pains are. Take amazing care of them. But don't put customers ahead of you like most business owners do. You'll end up drained, beat, defeated, and sad.

You'll start to resent your customers when it's actually your fault because you set the standard for how they interact with you. Take responsibility.

When you put yourself first and set up a business to take care of you, it creates a wonderful regenerative state. Self-love is important here.

I repeat: Set up a business to take care of yourself first. Do not let yourself be fooled, this can be done in any business category.

My favorite example is in the real estate industry. There was a Realtor who didn't want to work evenings or weekends. Most agents scoffed and laughed at him. They'd say, "You have to sacrifice your weekends with your family if you want to succeed in real estate!"

Determined to create his own life, he sat down and wrote out what he wanted.

He wrote, "I want to work 9 to 5, five days a week. I will not work weekends. And my phone will be off in the evenings to spend time with my family."

In a short period of time, the opportunity became clear. He started working with real estate investors 9 to 5. To get started with his customers, he'd tell the real estate investors: "Hey, my phone is off at 6:00 p.m. because I'll be with my family, and that's what I'd recommend you do too. Spend the evenings with those you love. If you call me, it will go to voicemail, but if you leave a message, I'll get back to you first thing in the morning."

Those Realtors who laughed at him quickly changed gears and started asking to learn from him. His wife and family were so happy to see he was never on his phone after 6:00 p.m. And he made a lot of money.

He ended up creating a course teaching Realtors this and making another six figure revenue stream teaching agents. All because he was a leader of his own life and obsessed over the business model.

Let me repeat; you should **obsess** over your business model until it takes great care of you. And you can do this in literally any industry. Here are the criteria for my most valuable businesses:

1.  Automated sales (people sign up without speaking to me).
2.  Recurring revenue (people pay me monthly for years).
3.  I sell tools (instead of providing a service).
4.  I get paid upfront.

Break any of these rules, and you'll sacrifice your ability to generate wealth.

Many categories fit this mold. Selling courses, membership websites, gym memberships, and also software as a service (SaaS) fit these four criteria. SaaS is the most valuable business category as of 2020, it is what set me financially free. And although I get many people wanting to build a SaaS right away, SaaS is not a good first business; you'll want to cut your teeth on something simpler first.

Most of my successful students did not get a big win on their first business… it was their second or third. Business takes practice. Let yourself build a few products and focus on learning along the way.

You know you are successful at this when you can create a business that takes care of you and fills you up but doesn't drain you. That's a pretty hard thing to do. Not many get there. Not because of lack of skill but because of improper training and focus.

Be careful of this thought: *I can't do this because of X, Y, or Z reason in my industry. My life has to be this way or that.*

If you find yourself saying something like this, you are fighting to keep suffering. It might be a worthwhile experiment to break the mold. Create a new wave.

What would a pleasurable life really look like?

Most of us don't focus on questions like... "How can I set this business up to take care of myself?"

Most of us just ask, "How can I get something working and successful?"

Then we forget ourselves. Don't do that ok?

Have fun with this! Between studying different income streams and seeing different business examples, you'll build a strong, profitable surveyor brain.

## ❂ Exercise to Build Your Surveyor Brain ❂

Practice the "Customer. Pain. Solution. Offer." exercise on one business per day for 30 days, and you'll have a completely new brain. You can do it on your drive to work. Do it with any business you drive by. And note that it's better to keep a journal and look at it often.

Your brain needs to build new mental structures to succeed,

My top students have dozens and hundreds of these examples in their minds.

# ●THE TILLER

*The tiller prepares the ground and finds the profitable seeds to plant.*

# CHAPTER 11:

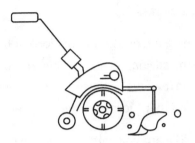

# THE TILLER

---

The tiller tills the ground and finds the seeds to plant.

If you master the ability to be a tiller, you'll never worry about money again. If you could only pick one brain to build, this would be the one to ensure financial safety.

_**Tilling**_ is akin to finding the person or niche market (the land) working with them to find the pain (seed you will plant) that will be solved for them.

I learned about the importance of finding pain from my dear friend Andrew Warner of Mixergy.com. He interviewed 750 entrepreneurs to find this pattern. I highly recommend you check out his site.

Tilling is a wild world. It's not as hard as you might think. And at the same time it can be difficult.

Many top entrepreneurs will resist hearing the true real pains, instead trying to force their own ideas upon a market—usually because they are an expert at something and are too insecure to venture out from their own area of expertise.

Or they are just too proud to listen.

And I'm talking about successful entrepreneurs too.

The ego is deadly. Remember, success is not about being right. It's about surrendering to what works.

For example, I've seen good entrepreneurs look at businesses doing very well and scoff at them, saying, "I can't believe this business works." Well, yeah, you can't believe it works because you're still ignorant. Because you have yet to understand that success requires surrendering to what works.

If it works, you should learn why with an open mind.

**The successful tiller is very humble.**

Have you ever wondered how a great business is really born? It's from an epic, sound, solid, powerful seed. The trick is that we don't look for the seed itself, instead, we look for pain.

The pain will reveal the seed.

Imagine that one afternoon you look over at your neighbors garden, and they have these amazing plants growing. They look gnarly and beautiful, straight out of the movie *Twilight*. With rich, deep colors. Standing tall and full of fruit.

You ask your friend, "Where did you get all those plants?"
And your friend looks over at you and smiles and says, "It's all about the seeds."

You were fixated on the plants. Wondering about them.

But really...
It's all about the seeds.
So many entrepreneurs. So many, try to fix a bad seed.

Don't try to fix a bad seed once it's growing above the surface. Don't try to change the plant itself. The seed of the idea is broken. Drop it.

For a seed to grow, it helps to be rooted within a deep pain. A real, deep pain.

Look at back pain, for example. People in serious back pain will spend over $50,000 on surgery to get better.

Or women who can't get pregnant. That pain is primal and awful. They will go to any length to solve it.

Or being single and alone. One of the biggest money-making niches online are folks at an older stage of life looking for a companion.

But then there are simpler ones that aren't so obvious, but still very painful. Like doing duplicate data entry when software could just automate that, getting clients to pay invoices on time, or being stuck in rush hour traffic.

I had a friend ask for advice about their business one day. They were doing $10,000 a month after four years of working on it. Yikes. After four years, they only earned $10,000 a month. And these folks were smart, doing all the right marketing.

They were doing everything right on top of a bad seed.

They asked me what to do. I shocked them when I told them, "Look...the seed is bad... find a new seed. Use the same customer base you already have, they already trust you. Talk to them. Find a new pain they have and build a better product with a better seed."

They have a huge advantage of a customer list who trusts them; they just need a new seed to sell.

Finding the seed can be a deep, involved process, but it can also be simple. The laundry detergent brand Tide had their employees come to homes and watch women do laundry. They found out that people had a hard time knowing how much detergent to put in. So they put a little measuring cup on top of the detergent. But then they came back and saw using the measuring cup became too messy.

Years later, the pre-measured tablets were born.

All from people watching moms do laundry in homes. Pretty simple.

## ❧ The Five Questions To Find A Painful Seed

Let's find a painful seed.

It's worth noting that **everyone has problems**. Even successful people. I still forget this so I'm telling you now. I'll often catch myself thinking, "oh, that person is successful they don't need my help."

But what's really going on is that I've held an identity that I'm unworthy of helping someone.

So I believed: "No one needs *my* help."

For this identity, I use what we teach in the earlier chapters to love and remove the trance of this thought, so I'm actually able to help someone. (See chapter six, face your mind).

Because here's what's incredible. The most successful people usually have the most diverse set of problems that are created from their success. And they are usually lonely in their success.

Unsuccessful people generally have basic problems. Things aren't working. And while those can be great, don't forget successful people in your sphere.

A successful person who has a 10 million dollar per year business is going to have many problems that need solved. They are so busy running a business they don't have the time to solve them all, and they are more than willing to pay for help.

I'm telling you this so you can focus on more groups of people. Everyone needs your help. Successful people, and unsuccessful. We all need help with something.

● My favorite repeatable process for finding these painful seeds is The Five Question Framework we use at StartFromZero.

● We call this "idea extraction."

Above all else, this process is nourishing and fun to do with someone because it's rather therapeutic. These five questions took us four years to compile and dial in. They are a combination of questions I learned from my mentors and personal experience that I put into a particular order.

I learned about finding pain from my friend Andrew Warner. I learned the other questions from a past mentor named Hiten Shah. I tested variations and came up with the following Five Question Framework:

1. Over the course of the last year, what has been your most persistent and present problem?
2. How do you currently go about solving that problem?
3. What happens if you don't solve that problem?
4. What would your dream solution be? (Or) If you could wave a magic wand how would you solve this problem?
5. Would that be worth paying for, and if so, how much?

It can really help to niche this down to a certain topic for the first question. You could ask what's your most persistent and present problem...

In the morning?
On your way to work?
Just before bed?
With your sleep?
While you're using your smartphone?
On Facebook?

Let's look at an example.

**Example #1:** The other day I asked my friend who was an online marketer...

1. *What's your most persistent and present problem right now?*
   *He said*: I was asked to do a guest blog post for a big website. So, I've been trying to finish it for a while, but it's long and draining.

2. **How are you going about solving it?**
   *He said:* By sitting here editing and re-editing. It's terrible. Draining. I like writing, but I can't stand editing.

3. **What happens if you don't get this blog post finished or solve this problem?**
   *He said:* All my work will be wasted, and I won't get any exposure. Which would be a colossal waste of time. (I loved that he said "colossal," LOL.)

4. **If you could wave a magic wand, how would you solve it?**
   *He said:* I'd just hand it off to someone and tell them to edit and finish it.

5. **Would that be worth paying for? If so, how much?**
   *He said:* Oh yeah, I'd easily pay $700 to $1000 if you found someone.

Now from there, I went to an online jobs website and found many great writers and editors (with good reviews) for him to hire and work with.

I posted something like this:

> *Wanted: Writers to Edit & Finish a Long Blog Post*
>
> *I have a blog post that needs to be edited and finished. It's around 1,500 words. If you can help, send me a message with links to your past work.*

Then I could link the two together. To help my friend out.

● I didn't come up with an idea. I just asked questions. I didn't have to be an expert; I found experts for him. I could pocket a finder's fee for connecting the two and be on my way to solving the next problem.

There are many online job websites to consider. You can strike gold, but depending on what you need some options are better than others. To see all my recommendations for job sites, visit StartFromZero.com/Yes—no email capture required.

Remember, business is fundamentally...

- Customer → Uses A Mechanism → To Get A Result

In this case it was...

- *Customer*: Online marketing friend.
- *Result*: A finished blog post.
- *Mechanism*: Hiring an editor.

I had a friend who wanted a finished blog post. I can hire out the mechanism.

Remember, look for real pain. Articulate it clearly like I have above. Once you've done this, you don't have to understand the mechanism needed to solve it, find an expert to create the mechanism.

Sometimes you can struggle to find ideas when you're first doing idea extraction. It might take practice and the right person to talk to. If you're asking someone who isn't driven to make things better in their life, it might be hard to elicit a pain from them.

People who are driven to make a change for something generally make better candidates.

Listen to someone who shares his experience of doing idea extraction.

> "First, it was not nearly as hard or as scary as imagined it would be. In fact, the whole process was, surprisingly, just as much fun as others have said it can be.
>
> I approached my conversations with an attitude of playful helpfulness. I told the two people I talked to that I didn't have any expectations other than just getting clarity on something that's troubling them.

Ideas came really easily as we opened up and playfully probed at the issue.

All the questions were equally straightforward to ask and work through. I found that the questions invoke the logical brain well, so it felt natural to ask the feeling-related questions as well.

My first conversation didn't yield a sellable product or service, but the person felt so much better just having talked through the issue that we both considered it a win and totally worth the time.

The second conversation did yield a viable idea. It's not some-thing I'm personally interested in pursuing, but it made for a good exercise!

After having two conversations with friends, I feel really excited and interested in getting out and talking with more people."

— Ben

You can see Ben had a great time doing idea extraction, and though he won't be using any of the ideas from the first conversation he had, he's getting his practice in. Ben had fun, and the people he talked to enjoyed themselves.

That's critical to note. *The people he talked to enjoyed themselves.* This isn't a "a way to manipulate others to get ahead." This process is nourishing for all involved.

Did you imagine finding painful problems would be nourishing? It sure beats racking your brain to come up with an idea. Plus you get the joy of serving someone this way instead.

Let's look at one more example from a first-timer...

"That was awesome. I organized an idea-extraction call with a prop-erty manager for apartments today. The call went for 15 minutes.

- I covered all five questions and still managed to ask some other good ones that came to me during the call.

- I've learned that you have to enter the conversation with nothing on your mind and just ask questions and listen. A great idea to me might be worthless to a market unless it solves their problem. Overall, stay present, ask questions, probe, and listen.

- I found the first question to be the easiest. It opens the conversation for discussion, which makes it easy to implement and sets the tone of the call.

- The fifth question was the hardest. Even though I'm not selling anything (yet), I still get a little bit uncomfortable when talking about price and what someone would pay for something.

    I had a bit of anxiety before the call. *Will I find a solution? Are they actually going to answer? Will they question my motives?* During and after the call, I felt great. I'm at ease and believe I have successfully found a pain point with a possible solution."                    — Aaron.

You see that Aaron had a good first call with a stranger right off the bat. He also found a possible idea to sell. You can start to see through these two examples just how powerful and abundant our world is with the skills of idea extraction under your belt.

The number of product ideas out there are infinite.

There will always be more pain to be solved with a product. This is largely because every new advancement brings with it newly needed products. Look at the iPhone and how much opportunity that brought. Apps, developers, physical products like cases. When Facebook released its API, how many apps were made?

Giants innovate and create big demand for new things. There will always be more opportunities to create.

**So many of us are intimidated by finding a good idea. But that burden is removed with this process. We shift our focus to asking the questions; the idea reveals itself.**

Let's look at the anatomy of finding an idea, and then a sale, in a really interesting niche, college admissions. Meet Andrea, an artist at heart who happens to coach parents on getting their children into highly competitive colleges.

She wanted a scalable idea so she could focus on her art.

She applied idea extraction on her favorite coaching clients. She talked to two different parents she knew who were big spenders, data-driven and strategic. Sounds like an ideal client? Big spender and data-driven. Yum.

During her first idea extraction call, she found critical information for a product idea.

Andrea asked, "What would your 'genie in a bottle' solution be for getting your child into college?" One of the parents told her, "Everyone knows about having a high GPA and getting good grades as a strategy to get in, but you have to innovate or your kids look like everyone else. I wish I had case studies of successful students who got into top schools."

*Could it really be that simple?* Andrea thought. *That's all they want?*

Andrea was very excited. She decided to schedule and present a two-hour webinar of student case studies for parents. She sold the product for $300. She sold it in advance before the product existed. She recorded the presentation so it became a product she could resell without spending her own time. The $300 was almost all profit because the information cost pennies to ship or produce.

Imagine her webinar being titled... "College Admission Case Studies: Everyone Knows the Basics. Here Are The Secret Strategies Students Really Use To Get Admitted."

She had been stuck exchanging time for money for a long time and she was intimidated by creating a product. But when she saw they just wanted case studies, she knew she could present that in one two-hour presentation that she could record and resell.

That's an easy product to create. **Passive income was five questions and one two-hour presentation away for Andrea.**

Could you really be that close to having an income-scalable product? It is freaky how fast this can go. In Andrea's case, she already had the expertise to make the product. This can be a great way to go for fast product creation. Rely on your own expertise. But if she didn't, she could have found experts with knowledge in this area and organized the content for a profit split.

I typically go 80% me 20% experts on content splits. They do nothing but teach; I do everything else. Everyone is usually pretty happy in that scenario.

Not having expertise can be scary and make you feel vulnerable. But it doesn't have to stop you.

I didn't have any expertise when I was starting out, so it was intimidating. When I asked real estate brokers about their painful problems, they told me about problems I didn't know how to solve, so I had to find experts with that knowledge.

Real estate brokers would tell me, "I have problems recruiting more Realtors. Can you help me?"

And I'd tell them with full honesty, "I have no idea how to do that. Can you tell me what you would do?" It turned out they knew exactly what they needed to do. They just needed help because they lacked the time.

So they told me what they wanted, and I found a way to do it by hiring experts.

It was a great way to cut my teeth and get started.
You'll see exactly how I created the solution in the next section!

Andrea transformed because of this process. Look at how Andrea has blossomed today because she built her entrepreneurial brain. Here's what Andrea is up to now...

> "Last fall, I wrote and directed my first full-length theater production, and, a few months ago, I received a literary grant from the City of San Francisco for a new play I'm writing and will produce and direct in March.
>
> To address the business end of things, I've put together a professional artists mastermind (something I wanted to do for years), and I am launching a peer-to-peer arts lab for writers, directors, and performers who want to be independent and entrepreneurial about developing their careers.
>
> My educational business is still going well, but I've chosen to tend to it without hustle so I can move forward in the arts."

What do you hear in Andrea's life now?

> The freedom to be herself.

And this brings up a critical point: Even if you don't stick with entrepreneurship you will always be better at everything else if you try and learn these skills, no matter what you decide to do.

Entrepreneurial skills are transferable to any field.

## Exercise to Build Your "Tiller" Brain

Practice The Five Question process on your friends for fun. I found it made a really fun dinner conversation.

Present it like this: "I'm learning an entrepreneurial process to find business ideas by asking about painful problems we all have. Can I practice the process on you as an experiment? It's really easy and fun. It's five questions and takes ten minutes or so."

Plus it gives you a chance to get to know your friends in a new way.

Let yourself practice over and over. Do this anywhere from 10 to 20 times. Let your first time be messy and uncertain. Keep at it. Do it over and over. You'll find some questions are harder than others at first. Don't do it with selfish intention. Do it to connect with a person. If you focus on the connection and do this repeatedly, the idea will eventually reveal itself.

Remember, you can repeat the same five questions with the same person in many different areas. Sleep, business, productivity, relationships, etc.!

A common question I get is, "Is it possible for an introvert to become successful at this?" The answer is, "Yes, absolutely." I've seen it happen many times. Many successful entrepreneurs are actually introverts who can switch on an intelligence when talking with a customer or speaking to a room.

They won't be the loudest person at the party. They are usually at home enjoying their work :-)

## THE PLANTER

*The planter is someone who can plant and grow seeds into profitable products.*

# CHAPTER 12:

# THE PLANTER

If you follow the steps in this section when you create a product, it will be extremely difficult to fail.

First let's go over the map, and then I'll show you how it works using examples.

## The Humble Product Creator.

*It's an art:* of stripping things away.
*It's a practice:* of co-creation with your customer.
*It's an intuition:* for finding what seems off and coming into alignment with it.
*It's an intention:* of humility and truly helping another.

Before we begin, picture this...

Let's say you've humbled yourself to serve a fellow human. You've sat with them and asked about their deep pains. You asked them about their "magic wand or dream come true solution."

You've got your idea. You've got the solution. You're going to improve their life.

Now you're presenting the product to them. And it's **your product.**

They are joyfully pulling out their credit card to buy it...from you. How would you feel at that moment? Making money by improving someone's life in a tangible way and seeing the real potential for your financial freedom?

You are worthy and capable of all of the above with hard work.

The planter is someone who can plant and grow seeds into profitable products. Planters don't just throw seeds around where they want. They honor the laws of nature. Humble product creation has its own set of rules.

To describe the planter I created a chart called the Humble Product Creator.

The high goals of the Humble Product Creator are to get the product built quickly, with limited financial risk, and to get results for the first group of customers with the product. The true planter has removed their ego from the process and works from a place of serving.

Planters may seem like wizards to others. But it is truly the process that makes them seem magical. They surrender to what works. This type is a little more complex, so I've broken this brain into four states, four goals, eight distinctions, and four killers.

(Always keep this in front of you as a printable poster at StartFromZero.com/Yes)

It's pretty overwhelming to do all of this your first time with your first product, which is why I recommend you start by solving one problem at a time, for one person.

Your goal is to refresh your mind as often as you need with these concepts when you start building the product. Even if you're only able to follow half of these concepts and steps, you will still do better than most.

Remember this: Your idea means absolutely nothing until it is fully realized and demonstrated.

# Making Great Products Quickly with Helathy Profits as the Humble Product Creator

## It's an...

| | | |
|---|---|---|
| ART | Of stripping away | What can be removed? |
| PRACTICE | Of co-creation | What's the customer think about this feature? |
| INTUITION | What wants to happen? | What do the energetics want to allow here? |
| INTENTION | Humbly serving | How can I stop proving myself and serve instead? |

## The 3 Goals

1  Get product built quickly
2  With limited financial risk
3  Get results for first users

## The 8 Distinctions

1  Align Product to Sweet Spot Desire of Customer
2  Prototype Vision for the Product
3  Get Buy In, Yes, or Money
4  Find Experts to Create the Product Vision
5  Test Concept for Results or Build Now if Confident
6  Structure the Deal for Limited Financial Risk
7  Create a Communication Loop so You're Informed
8  Does This Product Meet Your Goals?

## The 4 Killers

1  Does the Customer Currently Do the Activity Outside of the Product?
2  Does it Require a Great Change of Behavior to Use?
3  Is the Burden to Use the Product High?
4  Does it Deliver the End Result Clearly?

From The **Conceptual** Idea → **Through The Void** Most People Get Lost Here... → To The **Concrete** Result

Going from the conceptual to the concrete is a bridge that most do get across successfully.

**Here are the eight steps and distinctions to make a great product quickly with a healthy profit.**

1. Align your product to the C.P.S.O.
2. Prototype the vision for the product (could be with pen and paper).
3. Get buy-in, yes, or money from the customer.
4. Find experts to create the product vision.
5. Test the concept for results (without building it) or build now if confident.
6. Structure the deal for limited financial risk.
7. Create a communication loop so you're always informed.
8. Think about your goals and if this product meets them.

**Here are the four killers of a great product.** Ask yourself these questions. The correct answers are in parentheses.

1. Does the customer currently do this activity outside of the product? (Best answer: Yes)

2. Does it require a great change of behavior? (Best answer: No)

3. Is the burden to use the product high? (Best answer: No)

4. Does the product deliver an end result clearly? (Best answer: Yes)

These four killers can save your product's life.

If the customer does not currently perform this activity outside of the product, that means they will need to add a new behavior, which is not a safe bet. You want to make the things they already do easier, not give them new things to do.

If your product requires a great change in behavior, you're not safe.

If the burden to use the product is too high, you're not safe.

If the product delivers an unclear end result, you're in trouble with your marketing.

Let's go through two examples, one success and one failure. This will show you how to apply these eight steps and four killers.

**The first successful example is my product called Recruiting Ninja.**

You'll want to note a key point to the success of this product: This product followed the pattern of finding a pain from just one customer, solving it for them, and then scaling to others. It made starting less overwhelming. I didn't think of market size or growth, or write out a plan, I just put my head down and solved one problem for one person. That's where your transformation will happen—with the first customer you solve a problem for.

### Step 1 – Align Your Product With C.P.S.O.
*Customer*: Real estate broker.
*Pain*: Recruiting real estate agents. It is difficult to stay consistent.
*Solution*: An online recruiting system an office assistant can run for them.
*Offer*: $100 to $200 per month.

### Step 2 – Prototype the Vision for the Product
Don't complicate this. A prototype is just a sketch. I drew up a two-column website on a piece of paper (see below). I then posted a job on a marketplace for a designer, paid $350, and picked the best design. (See my best design recommendations at StartFromZero.com/Yes).

This was my drawing...

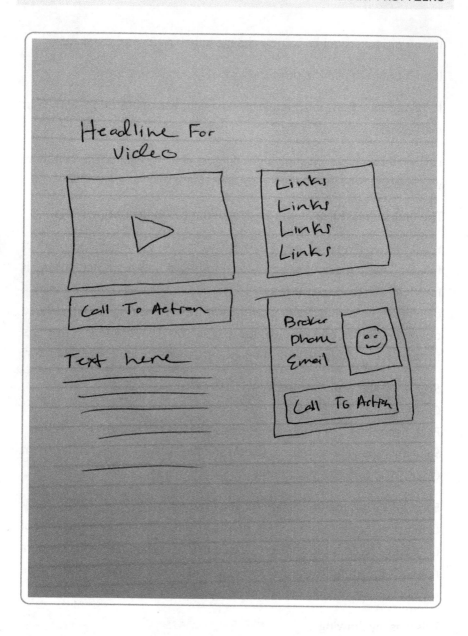

Became this, back in 2006!
(It's even missing the Macromedia Flash player).

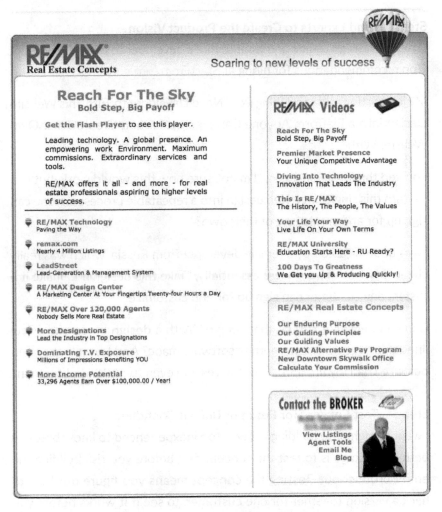

Isn't that incredible? Did you think design could be that easy? You just draw on a piece of paper and then hand it over to someone.

Once I got this design, I was ready for the next step. I had only designed one page as you can see.

### Step 3 – Get Buy In, Yes, or Money
I showed this picture to my uncle, who was a real estate broker. He said, "Yes." Because this was my first business, I was grateful to have my uncle because my confidence was low.

### Step 4 – Find Experts to Create the Product Vision

I used the design I made and went to hire a developer to build the product. (Top recommendations for hiring at StartFromZero.com/Yes.)

My job posting said something like, "Need Developer to Turn This Website Design Into a Platform Anyone Can Sign up for and Create Their Own Website With."

I posted the image and said, "I'm not sure how this would work, but can we turn this single page web design into a repeatable process anyone can sign up for and create one of their own?"

I was quoted $2200 by a female developer from Russia, which was really cheap. My instructions were essentially, "Take this design and make it a system any customer can sign up for and customize."

Can you believe it can be that simple? With a design made and a few lines of instructions, I was getting software made? And I wasn't as scared because I had my first customer say yes and even fund the development.

### Step 5 – Test Concept for Result or Build if Confident

I went straight into building it. I was too inexperienced to know better. A better way to go is to test the concept first before you risk building the entire product out. Testing the concept means you figure out how to hack a version together for one customer, to see if it works before you build it into a full-on system. You can Google "how to create minimum viable products" or "how to hack together a solution" for lots of training on this matter.

### Step 6 – Structure the Deal for Limited Financial Risk

I had very little cash. But instead of saying, "I can't afford it," I asked myself the famous *Rich Dad Poor Dad* question, "How can I afford it?"

The idea came to me to ask my uncle if he'd pay for the development. He did the math of paying $100 a month for life or just paying $2200 to get it free forever. He chose to fund my project and get it free for life. I was only 22 and extremely nervous. I was so grateful.

**Step 7 – Create a Communication Loop so You're Always Informed**
Since this was my first project, I had no idea about how to stay in contact, so I just waited for my developer to contact me with updates. It was pretty stressful. I wasn't sure of the progress much of the time. I felt in the dark. It was really hard not having control.

Today, I created a communication loop by having my expert email me every day the answers to four questions. I learned these 4 questions from a mentor of mine Eben Pagan.

1. How many hours did you work?
2. What did you accomplish? (Not what you did; what did you accomplish?)
3. What problems did you encounter?
4. What questions do you have for me?

This keeps me informed each day and much more confident about the direction of the product.

**Step 8 – Think About Your Goals and if This Product Meets Them**
My goal was to make $10,000 a month, so if I were to land one hundred brokers at $100 a month, my goal would be met. All went well; I had a few hiccups, but they were nothing major. With great marketing using my gardener brain, that product made me over $700,000 over the span of five years. On average, it brought in over $100,000 a year.

Now...let's talk about the downsides of this product. And why it eventually shut down.

# The Killers

**Killer #1: Does the customer currently do this activity outside of the product?**

I'd say maybe 10% of brokers consistently do recruiting. Most don't. They want it fully automated. The greatest products fully deliver the end result. They give something for next to nothing. Those are the greatest of products.

In other words, this would have been a better product if it delivered a recruited agent. The product only went halfway. It was a tech system they had to run.

**Killer #2: Does it require a great change of behavior?**

Yes. Many brokers weren't actively recruiting.

Remember...requiring new behavior is a scary "no-no" (anyone still using the NordicTrack?)

In this case, most brokers are not actively recruiting, nor are they doing it consistently. Brokers were trying to buy a result, and I was trying to get them to make behavior change. Because this was a new behavior for them, it was a risk. I didn't really get the value of this concept at the time.

The system was just a system. A broker still needed to promote it.

**Killer #3: Is the burden to use high?**

Yes, most brokers are not tech-savvy; in this case, they would set up the website and leave it. That's why I added a checklist their virtual assistants could use and that helped a lot.

**Killer #4: Does it deliver the end result clearly?**

Brokers wanted recruited agents. They wanted agents to contact them without rejection. This did help with that at times, but not all the way.

Recruiting success is a long-term game built on consistency and relation-ships; most brokers burn out doing it.

Without us doing the work for them, this product didn't last longer than five years. This product was great; it made me financially free as a young twenty-something, and I brought in over $100,000 a year for five years. But because of the issues listed above, it required my time to keep growing. Ultimately, it was not a sustainable business. Without continual marketing it would die off.

Now this industry is ripe for profit and value. If I would have taken the time to build a fully automated recruiting platform with websites, drip emails, text broadcasts, voice broadcasts, automated value-added webinars...it would have done extremely well. In this case, I would be doing more to deliver the desired result. However, my calling had changed, and I didn't want to fulfill this business.

In terms of deciding to pursue a particular product...pay attention to the killers.

**Let me tell you about a sneaky scary failure, clientlunchbox.**
I say sneaky and scary because it was the elusive fruit that gave a good first taste but never gave me the full fruit tree. They say passion is a critical component to success. No. I was passionate about this product.

But all the passion in the world can't save a faulty seed. Remember we do not get to decide what works.

Before we get into the breakdown, here's a little background. The idea for clientlunchbox started off as a review website for a Realtor's track record of selling real estate. It was Google reviews for a Realtor's history, before Google reviews existed.

I came up with it. It was cool. To me. But as I was talking to agents, they wanted help with their contact database. Not a review website. They hated their current database software.

I asked them what they hated about it. They said "logging in and remembering to use it." So to solve that problem I came up with a concept that worked like this... The product emailed you daily, requesting a reply if you had any new leads you'd like to add, with a list of all your other past leads you'd emailed in.

You could use it without logging in.

Here's an example of the email that would be sent.

*************Begin Email********************

Hi David,

Did you meet anyone new today that you'd like to add to your lunchbox? Just reply to this email and press enter to separate each piece of information. The data you enter will be automatically stored into your online database.

For example:

Name
Phone
Notes
Becomes...

Dillan Jones
5235555789
Met at Mexican restaurant

Reminder: You have three contacts that you have not done anything with yet.

1. Molly Monker, 5155347894, Met at coffee shop
2. Lindsey, Leeb, 1234567890, Starting at Wells Fargo
3. Dirk, Albright, 3216547890, Referral while birthday shopping

Make sure you remember to contact them or update their info.

- Login to your database–click here

Happy hunting,

Your clientlunchbox

**************End Email*********************

Agents would reply with a name, number, and a note. I showed this email and concept to agents, and they loved it. So, I pivoted from the reviews website. Then built it. Hired a developer. Recruited investors.

But I never asked them to pay right away. Oops.

At the end, we had around 21 paying customers, but over time Realtors stopped using it because in order to use it, they needed to be...consistent.

This was a new behavior for many Realtors, and they didn't adopt a new behavior. That's not their fault. New behavior is hard to create.

Let's dive into this example.

**Step 1–Align Your Product With a C.P.S.O.**
*Customer*: Real estate agents
*Pain*: Complicated contact database systems.
*Solution*: Email-based contact database
*Offer*: $9 to $49 a month

**Step 2 – Prototype the Vision for the Product.**
I did this well. Instead of drawing something on a sheet of paper, I made this prototype by telling a simple story. I wrote a five-day story in a Google

Doc about how an agent would use the product. "It was an early morning, and Bob the agent got an email from his contact database saying..." That sort of thing.

It was a great way of validating a product before building it or drawing anything—just tell the story of how a target customer would benefit from it. Let them read it. It's a powerful exercise. The story is quite long to read here, but you can see that full story at StartFromZero.com/Yes.

What I would have done differently here: Getting buy-in would have been great, but real-world application made all the difference. I could have run this email manually for one agent to see how it went. It didn't require software to test this. I would have just managed emailing each day for a few agents. This would have saved my arse.

I could have said, "Great, pay me and I'll do this manually with you for 30 days and lets see what happens. I'll be your email virtual assistant."

Imagine how quickly that could have figured things out.

### Step 3 – Get Buy-In, Yes, or Money.
I got great excitement from agents. But I was still new to entrepreneurship, so I didn't ask for any orders.

### Step 4 – Find Experts to Create the Product Vision.
I found a guy to build clientlunchbox on a Ruby on Rails Google group. Google groups were a secret place to find top talent without wading through a crowded job board. I sent this email to the top ten members in the group and found a great builder. Here's the email I sent to the developers:

> Subject: Impressed – want to hire you?
>
> Hi [NAME], I've been reading your posts on Google groups, and I am quite impressed.

I think you could really make my app fly. It's still in the planning phase, and I'd like to talk about hiring you. Rather than leave you completely in the dark before asking you to reply, I thought I'd tell you a little about it.

The App works like this. (Then I linked to the story I wrote).

What do you think?

—

Dane Maxwell

My phone number

**Step 5 – Test the Concept for Results or Build Now if Confident.**
I went ahead and built this with Jeff, my developer. But like I said, I could have tested this without ever having to build software first by just powering the email functionality myself with one or two agents.
But I was new.

**Step 6 – Structure The Deal For Limited Financial Risk.**
This developer I paid $50 an hour. It was going to get expensive.

Because the product was more expensive, I got my uncle and a friend to invest $9,000 each, or $18,000 total. It ended up costing $32,000 over one year. (Not to fear, folks, this was my most expensive product to get out the door.) With a little math, that means I spent $14,000 of my own money to get it built.

This was the most expensive product, for the smallest price point per month. Sounds intelligent right? Hah.

And the $32,000 wasn't all at once. It crept up over a year.

**Step 7 – Create a Communication Loop, so You're Always Informed.**
When trust is low at the start...to keep developers accountable...and

to keep you feeling sane about what they are doing...you can use Eben Pagan's four-question framework that I've mentioned.

I ran Eben Pagan's four questions diligently with the developer for clientlunchbox.

1.  How many hours did you work?
2.  What did you accomplish? (Not what did you do?)
3.  What problems did you have?
4.  What questions do you have for me?

I stored the entire conversation inside a Google Doc. It got pretty long. To keep us sane, I would talk using a blue background, and the developer would talk in red. One of my friends told me to build this concept of communication as a software product to manage developers instead of using Google Docs. I was too busy and declined.

The doc is gnarly. It will literally show you what it's like to build a software project from scratch up to the point of getting paying users. It includes a full marketing report with all the landing pages and emails I used, and the software development log. Those two things will give you a complete picture for what building a SaaS is like. If you'd like these documents you can pay for them at StartFromZero.com/Yes.)

### Step 8 – Does This Product Meet Your Goals?

My goals were greedy—to have a bigger niche market; that was about it. I was tired of my small, 2,800 person list when I had 60,000 Realtors I could be emailing. I thought the real estate broker/owner niche was too small. I just wanted to make a product Realtors liked. I knew I'd profit if it worked because the model was software as a service.

In the end, the business didn't work. My uncle was cool with the loss. He understood the investment, but the other investor was pretty upset. He thought I gave up on the product. But I worked harder on this one than any other product. Eventually, though, I found that the seed was bad and chose to exit. I sold clientlunchbox for $3,000 on an auction and gave the investors each half and ate my loss.

Now let's talk about the killers for this product.

### Killer #1: Does the customer currently do this activity outside of the product?

Some Realtors would keep track of clients on a legal pad. Most would do nothing. So that seemed OK.

### Killer #2: Does it require a great change of behavior?

Agents checked email, so I figured they could reply and store their contacts. (But no, it was still too much of a burden for them to even use email for a contact database consistently.)

Simply because most agents don't think like business owners, and I don't blame them.

### Killer #3: Is the burden to use high?

No, at least I thought. They didn't have to login anywhere, so it was great, but what I didn't know is that they found email to be a burden.

### Killer #4: Does it deliver the end result clearly?

It helped them keep track of their clients. If they used it, it worked well. Realtors would save deals because of it. Interestingly, a Realtor called to tell me he saved a $6,000 commission with the product by remembering a lead. But then he would not pay $9 a month to keep using it.

He made $6,000. But would not pay $108 a year for that to happen again.

Yeah, that got to me. Maybe the product was cursed. LOL.

In cases like this, it is never advised to resent or be angry with the customer. Let curiosity guide you. Do not force a flower to bloom.

So, here's where it went wrong. It required agents to use it consistently. I got validation, I got leads, I got paying users, I got results. But at a low price point. That was hard.

And also... *It wasn't viewed as a critical component to their business.*

Realtors needed deep business training to understand the value of a contact database. Most Realtors didn't know if they had five hundred contacts that they kept in touch with consistently, they would sell on average 14 deals a year because that's how often people move. (Those are the standard stats).

No prospecting. No new leads. No risking money on advertising. Just staying in touch with five hundred people. But most Realtors (and humans, for that matter) are not consistent. It required a mindset change for many to become business owners and care about things like a contact database.

One year later, I found something that made me laugh hard (after punching a wall). I found out the top 10% of Realtors already used a contact database. The agents complaining were in the bottom 90% of producers who didn't really run their business like a business. What I think this subsect of Realtors were saying when they wanted an easier contact database was... "I don't want to grow up and become a business."

Another issue to consider: this product did not follow the pattern of finding a pain from one customer, solving it, and scaling to others. Doing that first would have saved me a lot of trouble.

Also...

**It was a concept most of the time.** Remember when I said your ideas are worth literally nothing as concepts until they are demonstrated and proven? Yeah, it's true.

This product was a lot of fun to work on, but it had disappointing results. I spent around $32,000 on it and lost around $9,000 of my own and

$18,000 of my investors' money. The peak revenue was maybe $800 a month. So I made a little money back on the recurring revenue.

But I'm grateful for this experience because my future products have made me millions because of this education.

We all pay tuition, folks :-)

The Planter is such a critical "brain" to take the time and build, and it requires a lot of heart and humility. If you are able to masterfully learn these skills and practice while building your confidence, one day you could build remarkable products.

## In Regards to Finding Experts to Build Your Products

People over complicate this.
If you're looking for an author to write a book...

Go to Google and search "how to hire a writer for a book."

If you're looking for a software developer...

Go to Google and search "how to hire a software developer."

If you're looking for someone to make you a skateboard...

Go to Google and search "hire an engineer to make a skateboard."

Remember that you're the one with the customers, the idea, and the end result the customers all want. That makes you the owner. The product is *maybe* 25% of the business, which is why we build it after we get the idea proven, not before.

You can also see my top recommendations for job boards at StartFromZero.com/Yes.

## In Regards to Getting Results for Your First Users

This part is pretty simple; give them the product and **watch them use it.** Don't send over a link to something and wait in the dark; get on a screen share and watch them see it for the first time. Keep tweaking until it makes sense to them, until they can actually use it, and it generates a result. In reality this could take a few attempts and tries at the product. So give yourself the time and space required.

As a humble product creator you will be doing this...

> Find Pain → Sell Pain → Find Expert → Get Solution Made → Watch Customer Use → Tweak Until Results Happen.

## Here's an Exercise to Build Your "Planter" Brain

Look at the chart we have designed in this section and draw out the map by hand a few times on paper with a blue pen. Blue pens activate a crazy amount of neurons and facilitate retention. This will be life-changing for you to do, slowly.

This is the secret to building pattern recognition triggers in your brain. Repetition and presence with the activity.

Then read the two examples in the "Planter" section above after you've drawn out the visual map by hand. Looking at the two just after copying the map will really drive this concept home into your subconscious brain.

After that, you'll really know this section and be prepared to implement it because it will be deep within your mind. The next time you build your own product, or you hear someone talk about their own product idea, you'll be able to help make it a success.

Also it might be a good idea to download the picture diagram for free at StartFromZero.com/Yes.

I struggled with what business examples to fit into this section of the book.

I wanted to show you this process with a dangerously close product so you don't make a mistake like I did with a close call that should never actually be built. With that being said, if you'd like to see another breakdown of my most successful business, PaperlessPipeline, and how it fits into these categories, visit StartFromZero.com/Yes.

## THE GARDENER

*The gardener knows how to grow revenue streams like a garden.*

CHAPTER 13:

# THE GARDENER

The role of a Gardener is to grow healthy plants. The Gardener performs a range of general maintenance tasks. This type helps you grow your product revenue, but only after you have a product that has delivered results to your first customer.

As a Gardener, I want to give you the simplest path I know to grow product revenue, which is to focus on the following:

1. Get the concept tested or built.
2. Get it into the hands of your first customer.
3. Get that first customer a result (treat them with the care of a newborn baby).
4. Repeat with your next few customers.
5. Get all of your customers' results.
6. Document the results as case studies and stories.
7. Create one focused marketing process using your case studies to convert paying customers.
8. Promote the case studies within the niche market. (Tip: Master a single traffic source first, before you expand.)

This might sound like a lot of steps, so let me share a few examples to illustrate how they work. Let's start with a company called The

OnlineListingMachine. I loved this business because I didn't force it. It came to me as a side idea from the action I was taking on other businesses.

After I built the Recruiting Ninja product, one of my customers had the clever idea to use her recruiting website as a system to get more home listings instead of recruiting agents. She called me up and said, "Hey, Dane, can I buy another recruiting website and use it to get real estate listings instead of agents?"

"Sure!"

I hung up the phone, set up a second recruiting website for her, and forgot about it. Eight months later, she contacted me to tell me what happened. She had done so well with this idea that she had gotten 80 listings to sell in that time period. That's a lot of listings!

She had gotten 80 listings in eight months.

Word on the street is that the average Realtor gets five listings a year or so.

Let's go through the eight steps.

1. **Get the product built.**

   That was done. The recruiting product was built. A customer just needed to change a few words to apply to real estate listings instead of recruiting.

2. **Get it into the hands of your first customer.**

   This was already done. She had it.

3. **Get that first customer a result.**

   This was done; she had gotten 80 listings in eight months.

4. **Repeat with your next few customers.**

   This is where I finally came in. Once my first customer had the result, I had to redesign the product for others to use. I had my developer take the code for our recruiting product, reproduce it, and changed the wording so it worked for real estate listings. Same product. Same template. Different wording used to "recruit listings" instead of "recruiting agents." Once I did this, I got five more clients to test the product.

5. **Get all of your customers' results.**
   In three months' time, four out of five customers produced results with the product. Not as good as the first customer with 80 listings, but good enough for me to move forward.

6. **Document the results as case studies and stories.**
   I interviewed each of these customers and had five case studies I interviewed that documented results.

7. **Use a single marketing process to sign up paying customers.**
   I followed the Product Launch Formula by Jeff Walker to launch this business (links to his books and courses at StartFromZero. com/Yes), which I recommend. In essence, I had a landing page promising Realtors a system for getting more listings, leading to a series of five customer case studies demonstrating proof, ending with a link to a program details page for them to buy.

8. **Promote those within the niche market (best to master one source of traffic first).**
   I acquired an email list of agents and promoted their stories for the next four weeks.

By the end of the four weeks, I had signed 40 Realtors to a $200-per-month product and built an $8,000-per-month income stream. I made around $50,000 in total before I essentially shut it down.

It wasn't worth the work in the end.

My first six customers were all owners of real estate companies who thought like business owners. Selling to most Realtors is very different. Many don't have the business owner mindset.

The product required someone who could run a system.

Although I folded the business in the end, I still consider it a great learning experience and success. I had a product that got someone a result. I found more people to test the result. Then I moved forward to launch the business.

Start small. Focus on one customer, then slowly expand, mastering one source of traffic.

Let's look at these eight steps for my next business, The Foundation! (Now called StartFromZero)

1. **Get the product built.**
   I wanted to teach people how to build software businesses—to launch a course. It was just an idea.

2. **Get it into the hands of your first customer.**
   I was being interviewed on Mixergy.com about my business PaperlessPipeline.com—I made an offer at the end of my interview to teach others.

3. **Get that first customer a result. (Treat them with the care of a newborn baby).**
   Around 2,200 people watched the interview, 240 applied, and then eighty-eight people accepted the offer. Really good numbers. Out of 88 students, only 30 completed the entire training, and 10 students succeeded in creating products!

4. **Repeat with your next few customers.**
   I used the customers' results as case studies to launch the next training. The cash was great, but it wasn't a strong asset, as it

required my time. I would never have created this business if I
hadn't built a software asset growing in the background at the
same time.

5. **Get them all the results.**
   Of these next 336 students, we had around 70 who started a
   business and made their first sale starting from scratch. We got
   a lot better at teaching.

6. **Document the results as case studies and stories.**
   We went bigger and launched again.

7. **Create one focused marketing process to convert paying customers.**
   We had one simple funnel, a landing page video, a case study
   video after the prospect entered an email address. But there was
   only one funnel that the prospect moved through to buy. These
   are my favorites. Just one way to move forward.

8. **Promote the case studies within the niche market (Tip: Master
   a single traffic source first, before you expand).**
   We promoted and launched this entire business on one major
   traffic source: podcast interviews.


This is a great way to start a business. It makes building a business easy.
And I had peace of mind with this process. My attitude is that if it works,
great, and if not, it's no big deal.

I didn't force a tree to grow on a rock. I gave these businesses time
to unfold.

There are plenty of individual tactics to grow a business, but this is a strategic
process and will work well on any platform or with any tactic you choose.

The challenging trick is to find one traffic source that works and make full
use of it in every way. That takes a little courage and experimentation.

You could run Facebook ads, host webinars, run Google Ads, promote on YouTube, or write guest blog posts on popular blogs in the niche space. There are many options. The important thing is to share your customers' positive results and stories on those channels.

And to use discernment for the best channel at the time. Back in 2008 that was email marketing. Then in 2013 it was the podcast segment. Now it's mastering the news feed or cranking YouTube ads correctly.

It's pretty normal to feel fear when starting out on a new marketing channel. This is oddly tricky. First, you have to find one source that works. Second, you have to be smart enough to know it's working and not dilute your focus elsewhere (I speak from experience).

Business becomes complicated when you start doing all the things you *think* you need to do. Let's just come to the understanding that 95% of all business owners have no idea what they are doing. That means you should not look at them, model them, or do what they say.

Imagine the simplicity and peace you'd have if you thought the following: "I'm going to find someone with pain, help them get a result with an expert, then find a few more people, help them get results, then I'm going to tell their stories to others in the same niche and build my business on one traffic source, just to get started."

This is the way this process works. Everything else you do beyond this is a waste of time. That's all you need to focus on. It's so powerful and profitable. Your bank balance will climb.

The most startling thing about growing product revenue is seeing what you do *not* need. You *don't* need a fully functioning website. Or a complicated funnel. I've had friends tell me they make $30,000 per month and they don't even have a website. They just find audiences online and promote webinars to them, telling stories of results in those webinars and asking others if they want to use the same mechanism to get the same results. And I'm not talking about the shady webinars. I'm talking about the legit ones.

I didn't have a website for The Foundation until after we had made $150,000. We ran on Google Docs and a Slack chat room. I did not have a marketing website for PaperlessPipeline until we had 16 paying customers. We had a hidden URL for people to login.

*All I spent my time doing was getting customers into a product and helping them get results.*

Let me show you one last example of growing product revenue. When I wanted to start my first business, all I needed was to get my first sale, then I'd believe in myself. I built my first product called the AgentCareCenter. com, now called MyAgentBase.com. It was an intranet (which is an internal company website) that organized files, private discussion, links, and a calendar for the agents of a real estate office. I didn't come up with the idea; I discovered it by hearing the pains of real estate company owners.

At the time I was an intern at my uncle's real estate company.

During a meeting one day, my uncle was telling his Realtors, "OK, first you need to do *this*, then *this*, then *this*, then go *here*, find *this* website, go *here*, and do *this*."

One of the agents raised his hands and asked, "Do you have a single place we can go to find all this information?"

My uncle shrank a little and said, "No."

And in those two sentences, and hearing my uncle's reply, the seed for the AgentCareCenter was born. A seed based on pain. As soon as I got my uncle a result, I used that example to get another customer, and then another.

The example told as a story was dead simple because I didn't even understand the nuance of copywriting yet.

**Here's My $250,000 Email Template.**

This email template is responsible for generating roughly $250,000. I sent out emails like this when I was just getting started (not exact, but very close).

> Subject: Would you like one of these?
>
> Have you ever heard of Robb Spearman? He's a RE/MAX owner in Iowa who just set up his very own AgentCareCenter for his agents.
>
> Here's what it looks like.
>
> Robb was really happy with it. He just finished telling me...
>
> "My agents love the AgentCareCenter. It organizes everything they need to do business in one place, and best of all, it gives me an easy way to communicate with them."
>
> If you'd like one of these sites or want to know pricing, just reply, and I'll help you get one set up.
>
> If not, I hope you enjoy your day!
>
> Thank YOU,
>
> —
>
> Dane Maxwell
> Phone
> Company name

Here's what this pattern is:

> Subject: [Direct personal question]
>
> Have you ever heard of [customer name]? They are x from y who just setup [product name].
>
> [Insert direct link to specific result].

[Customer name] was really happy with it. They just finished telling me...

[Insert customer testimonial that also addresses your target markets pain in the testimonial].

[Insert call to action with link to setup or reply to request more info].

[Positive sign off],
[Name]

After seven years, The AgentCareCenter has made an average of $3,000 a month. That's $36,000 a year in extra income. That's around $252,000 in total. And that's $3,000 a month with only 30 customers. The lifetime value of these customers is high—one customer has paid me over $16,000 for AgentCareCenter.

Remember, I didn't come up with the idea. I didn't spend any of my money to get it built. I did it following the same process I've used to grow revenue for every successful business. You can do this too if you take the time to learn.

Once your product works, holy crap is it cool. Once you get your first customer the result they want, your life changes completely.

How do you grow product revenue? By getting results for your first customers and using the results as stories in a single marketing channel as you grow, funneled into a single marketing sequence.

**This Works Because...** *Selling Proof* **Works.**

There is no better marketing mechanism I've found than demonstrating proof. That's why you work so hard to get results with your first few customers.

Start small—get a result for one person. Document the result. Promote it to others who are similar.

## Exercise to Build Your "Gardener" Brain

Start looking at proof marketing online and off. Find marketers smart enough to lead with results. Gardeners focus on using the proof and results of their customers to run their marketing. Pay attention to other businesses that are using this method, too.

Weight Watchers is an excellent example. Look at this piece:

**Oprah congratulates members on their success**

Like Jen, who lost 72 lbs*

*People following the WW program can expect to lose 1-2 lbs/wk.

`More member stories`

Create an email account to sign up to marketing lists from top marketers who lead with results. Study these emails not to buy but to learn.

Of all the points you could lead with, results will almost always be best. So, work hard to get your first few customers those results. I have links and resources on how to set up simple funnels at StartFromZero.com/Yes.

# That's it. Can you see how the four brains will help you?

**First**, learn to see the world in income streams (the Surveyor).

**Second**, learn where to find seeds (ideas) and prepare the soil (the Tiller).

**Third**, learn how to plant seeds (the Planter).

**Fourth**, learn how to garden and grow the ideas (the Gardener).

Many successful entrepreneurs don't have all four traits. You can usually get away with having just the first two. But if you combine all four, you'll be superhuman in your ability to generate profits.

# FIND YOUR NEXT IDEA HERE

## First, Watch Me Find a Great Business Idea in Ten Minutes, Then Do It Yourself.

Abundance is everywhere. It truly is, and you're about to see this firsthand.

This experiment will turn the lightbulb of abundance on within your mind.

Throw yourself into this experiment, and I believe it will change your life. You don't have to believe me. Read this section and then decide for yourself.

As I've said, many people think we need to be brilliant or work hard to come up with an idea. Nah! Just sit with someone and ask these five questions.

Now let's get started finding your first seven business ideas. Note: you will do this process just to find ideas. Don't worry about solving the problems; just work on finding the ideas for now.

Your goal here is to ask these five questions to one person a day for seven days. It takes 10 minutes or less. You can ask your friends, partner, parents, anyone you like.

Every time you do this process, you build your entrepreneurial brain. And that's a nice brain to have.

Write down the customer, pain, solution, and offer for each conversation. This is the framework we learned in the previous section that makes up an income stream.

Here's a quick example of the process I did with my pregnant partner just weeks before she was ready to give birth. What a fun time for us both!

We were both sitting in the living room watching Silicon Valley on a Tuesday morning when I decided to try it out (I really love the freedom to sit around on a Tuesday).

I hit pause on the TV remote and asked, "Hey, can I ask you five questions real quick to try out a framework for my book?"
"Sure!"
I got started right away.

**What is your most consistent and present problem today?**
"Overcoming nausea."
I asked her if she could tell me more about that because it was a little vague. Understandably—she's in pain.
"I don't feel well, but I want to be able to finish my organizing projects today."
OK, that's good enough. Moving on to question two.

**How are you going about solving this problem right now?**
Initially, she said she was just avoiding it. But after a moment, she said, "Well, I've been trying different things, like eating and drinking water, putting my hair up, and taking a 30-minute nap. My hope is that one of these ideas will work, and maybe I can get up and do the work."
OK that's specific enough. Onto question three.

**What happens if you don't solve this problem?**
"Well, the house stays messy, and I have to do it tomorrow."
Good, but this left me with some doubt, so I asked a follow-up question out of curiosity because her pain didn't seem that severe, and I wondered if she'd want to even pay to solve it...

**"So how painful is this problem for you on a scale of 1 to 10?"**
"Right now, it's a three, but I know it will get worse if I let things keep building up."

Low pain, may not be good enough, but onto question four.

**If you could wave a magic wand, how would you solve this problem? Remember, it's a magic wand.**
"I would not be nauseous," she said with a smirk.
OK, great. That's obvious. Let's jump to question five.

**Would that be worth paying for? If so, how much?**
"Yeah, you know if there was a droplet or something I could take, and it would cure my nauseousness, and it was safe for pregnancy, I'd pay for that. I'd pay $25 for a bottle."

Out of curiosity, I asked her if she'd pay $50.

"No, I'm cheap!" (Her fists raised in the air, and she smiled). "Well, maybe if there was nothing else on the market. I could see other women paying $50 for more severe nausea, though."

Then after that, we moved on, and a few minutes later, she came back...

"Actually, yeah, I would pay $50 for the convenience of a droplet because I could go make ginger tea, but that is too inconvenient. I'd love to have a droplet."

Then she went to go make some tea because that was a new idea she had come up with. Hah! Great. Love this process!

OK, so we've done the experiment. Here's what I wrote down.
Customer: Pregnant women in the third trimester.
Pain: Nausea interfering with her day.
Solution: A droplet she can take in a bottle.
Offer: $25 to $50 a bottle, depending on the discomfort. Looks more like $50.

Now I've got my problem and my idea. That is all you need to do. I have an entire potential business I could start from five questions.

Just for your education, here's what I would do next if I pursued this. I could search for all kinds of solutions or generic remedies I could turn into potions. I could contact acupuncturists or naturopaths and partner with them on creating a solution. To promote this business I could run ads on the What To Expect sites and all the pregnancy apps.

Then, and you don't need to do this yet, but because my brain has been trained, and I can't help myself, here's what else I would do: I'd turn every woman into a promoter by giving them each a link to share their story of curing nausea so they can make affiliate income as well during pregnancy. This helps pregnant women with nausea and provides an income for their upcoming child.

Everyone gets better all around, and I have a great marketing source.

Look at this. I've already got a great business with potential.

Now, this is important. I would not look at competitors for very long, if at all; I would just go to work creating my solution, helping women, and talking to them instead. I don't like looking for competition because it scares me out of action. I like staying with my customers instead. I think a lot of people go into research mode and then paralyze themselves. **Stay focused on what keeps your business moving forward; there's always room for another excellent solution.**

The unknown makes many people nervous. Just moving forward without knowing everything is often very scary. But, it's important to get used to "doing." The more insecure you are in business, generally, the more you are tempted to research. Break that habit. Take action instead. Trust you'll be OK.

On a random note: I love the niche of women in the third trimester of pregnancy, but knowing women get nausea in the first trimester too, I'd just target all pregnant women.

This is only one idea, from one day, from one conversation. What will you find in your seven-day experiment?

**Now It's Time to Turn You Loose!**

Fill out these next seven conversations and watch your mind transform.

To get started with people, set the context and make your request for a conversation this way:

"Hey, I'm doing a process right now that helps me find awesome business ideas by asking about others' biggest problems. Would you mind if I tried the process out with you for fun to see what we find? It takes five to ten minutes."

I've found this is a really fun way to connect with people.

Then ask the five questions.

1. What is your most persistent and present problem today (or this week, month, year)?
2. How are you going about solving that problem now?
3. What happens if you don't solve it?
4. If you could wave a magic wand or have a dream solution, how would you solve it?
5. Would that be worth paying for? If so, how much?

Then input the answers into these fields below:

Day 1
Customer:
Pain:
Solution:
Offer:

Day 2
Customer:
Pain:
Solution:
Offer:

Day 3
Customer:
Pain:
Solution:
Offer:

Day 4
Customer:
Pain:
Solution:
Offer:

Day 5
Customer:
Pain:
Solution:
Offer:

Day 6
Customer:
Pain:
Solution:
Offer:

Day 7
Customer:
Pain:
Solution:
Offer:

Please share your results with our community at StartFromZero.com/Yes.
We can't wait to meet you!

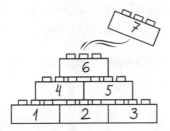

# THE SEVEN BUILDABLE SKILLS

## How to walk in a garden of wealth that belongs only to you.

What would you do with your own garden of wealth? Imagine having so much fruit that you could invite all of your friends over and share it with them. Imagine all of the contributions you could make to those you love if you had ample and abundant wealth.

People sometimes think I'm unusual because of what I've accomplished. They even ask me questions as if I have a magical answer. What they don't understand is...

Without these business skills, I'm just a dude with a dream. I guess what I'm saying is, I worked hard to acquire the proper skills, and people call it magic.

It's not magic. It's very predictable.

These skills help you build your own garden of wealth. You can build all of these skills at once, or one at a time, but **you'll need them all**. These skills are hidden from most people.

You can show someone these skills, and they might even roll an eye, thinking they are too basic. But those who understand these skills cherish and value them like the holy grail that they are.

**Once you understand these skills, you'll start walking with wealth instead of reaching for it.**

CHAPTER 14:

# USING WORDS THAT SELL

Using words that sell is the only skill you'll ever need to make money.

Think about this: if you only had the skill of using words that sell, you could just help sell other people's products without making your own and take a cut.

This powerful skill is remarkable. It allows you to...

- ◆ Multiply your sales in the printed word, breaking the time-for-money gap.
- ◆ Speak in ways so others will never forget you and follow.
- ◆ Create even better products in your customer's mind.
- ◆ Recruit top experts into your business because you know how to speak to their hearts.
- ◆ And also, hold attention for longer periods of time.

What is this skill?

Marketers refer to this skill as the master skill of copywriting.

What is copywriting? Technically speaking, copywriting is salesmanship in print. But actually, copywriting is Thor's hammer in business. Let's look at an example. In just 10 words, Domino's Pizza became a billion-dollar company.

What did they say?

Hot, fresh pizza delivered in 30 minutes or it's free.

This is not an accidental sentence. It is built on the most time-tested formula used by the smart few. And it made Domino's a billion bucks.

Weight Watchers has often used the same formula...

Lose 10 pounds in a week, or your money back.

And then real estate agents caught on, and you'd see them saying...

Your home sold in 90 days, or I'll buy it!

This powerful formula can be used for any business. This time tested formula is...

[End Result a Customer Wants] + [In a Specific Period of Time] + [Addressing Objections]

You could go out right now and help a friend's business by plugging in the right words and then slapping them on the top of their website. So many businesses would benefit from using this headline.
Imagine a chiropractor...

Your back or neck will feel better, or the session is free!

I'd definitely go to that chiro.

The power of copywriting is immeasurable. Why does copywriting create a billion-dollar pizza company? Because a good copywriter will speak to the deep pains and deep desires of the customer and then solve them immediately. This helps you to create better products.

Because you understand people.

I've used copywriting to write better emails in order to hire top software developers for my projects. Let me show you what I do. Here are the top pains and desires of a software developer.

- Pain: Unclear software projects that stress them out.
- Pain: Not being paid on time.
- Pain: Not working on projects that see the light of day.
- Pain: Not being respected for their talents and treated like mules.

I went out to the top developer communities and hired the best people I could find. The best employees are usually not looking for work, they are busy, so I go to them. After I find them, I write my emails with something like this:

> Subject: I really respect what I've seen
>
> Hey there, I really respect what I've seen you building online, so I thought I'd take a chance and reach out.
>
> I've got a software project I'm working on with really clear specifications and a vision, and I was wondering if you'd like to see it?
>
> I understand payment can be delayed on many software projects, so I'd be sure to pay you within 48 hours of you sending the invoice.
>
> This project has customers ready and waiting to use it, as well.
>
> Let me know if you'd like to hear more?
>
> —
>
> Dane

In this email, we've touched on each pain. Copywriting is powerful and can be used everywhere.

Even on your friends, partner, or children!

You could ask your partner, "Hey, can you tell me what would be the most important thing to you in having a great night with me?"

Your partner might say, "Just being able to spend time with you." (Of course they would say that.)

Then you'd ask, "Are there activities that help you feel the most connected to me?"

They might say, "I really enjoy watching movies and dancing with you. It's
a great combination!"

So then you'd say, "How would you feel if we went out to a movie and
then went dancing tonight?"

"That would be wonderful, but I have to be up early in the morning."

Now you have what we call an "objection" in copywriting: they have to be
up early. This time you ask the question while addressing the objection.
You'd say, "How would you feel about going out dancing and to a movie
with me tonight if we planned to get home early and didn't stay out late?"

Unbeknownst to her, you've just used another great copywriting formula.

[How Would You Feel if You Got] [Insert Desire 1] & [Insert Desire 2],
[Instantly], [ While Addressing Objection]!

You might already do this naturally. In that case, did you know you were
already a copywriter?!

Remember, copywriting is salesmanship in print. A thousand little sales-
people going out into the world and selling your product for you, through
your written words.

Copywriting is a vast topic, and you can find a large collection of copywriting formulas online by Googling copywriting swipe files, top copywriting
formulas, or top copywriting headline examples.

I have a very popular copywriting checklist you can download for free at
StartFromZero.com/Yes that includes 10 top patterns.

To learn copywriting on a deep level, read the following books:

  ◆ *Breakthrough Advertising* by Eugene Schwartz

- *Scientific Advertising* By John Caples
- *My Life In Advertising* By David Ogilvy

You learn copywriting by learning the language, learning the patterns, learning the frameworks, and looking at the best examples you can find. My friend Mike over at Swiped put together a resource of all the best sales letters as a bonus for this book at StartFromZero.com/Yes.

## Here's Your Exercise for Building Thor's Hammer, Copywriting.

Your opinion is not what makes money. Results make money. Study the things you know generate results, not the things you like. Read successful examples of top converting ads at StartFromZero.com/Yes and look for patterns.

Read one new ad a day for just one month and watch your copy-writing brain start to turn on.

# CHAPTER 15:

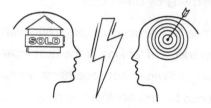

# OWNERSHIP VS. EXPERT THINKING

Expert or owner? When done correctly, the difference in wealth and income is substantial.

There is so much money to be made when you do things right.

Ownership is a safer path than being an expert, if you are trained and knowledgeable.

I went to the Boys and Girls Club for a short stint at teaching them wealth one day.
   "What do you want to be when you grow up?" I asked the boys and girls.
   "A basketball player!"
   "A rapper!"

Yikes.

Their brains were a product of what they saw on TV. That's called conditioning, or television programming.

I wanted them to grasp the power of being an owner versus an expert. T.V. teaches us to become experts. An expert sets out to learn skills they can use to exchange their time for money. An owner sets out to create or buy assets earning money while they sleep. They think very differently. It can be an uncomfortable transition to make until you realize it's not.

Next I asked them a question my first mentor asked me... "Would you guys rather be Michael Jordan or the owner of the Chicago Bulls?"

"Jordan!"

"Jordan!"

"Jordan!"

They all wanted the glory of being Michael Jordan on TV. Understandably. The dude is a legend.

Then I asked them, "So, if you're Jordan and you injured your leg, could you still play?"

"No..."

"Right, and if you couldn't play, would you still get paid?"

They had to think for a minute. You could really see them picturing the scenario. "Well...no...you'd need to play to get paid." You could see wheels turning. They were starting to get it.

"OK...now if you owned the Chicago Bulls and you injured your leg, would you still get paid?"

Silence for a moment. Then they spoke up. "Well, yeah, we would still get paid...because it doesn't matter if you're hurt or not. The team can still play."

"Right. So if you could be the owner of the Chicago Bulls, or Michael Jordan, who would you want to be?"

All of them unanimously answered...

"Owner!"

"Owner!"

"Owner!"

"Are you sure? Playing basketball could be fun."

"Yeah, we're sure. Well just play basketball for fun."

Mission accomplished.

Here is a little data on ownership verse expertise in basketball.

I did a little research and found that the average NBA player makes around $3,000,000 per year. And the average NBA Owner makes a minimum of $12,000,000 per year. That makes being an owner four times more lucrative in the NBA.

But those are just averages for the NBA.

> "The average small business actually generates about $100,000 in **revenue per employee**. For larger **companies**, it's usually closer to $200,000. Fortune 500 **companies** average $300,000 **per employee**. Oil **companies** generate over $2,000,000 in **revenue per employee**." —SmallBusinessMattersOnline.com

If you're an employee what you want to consider is if you make $35,000 to $50,000 a year, the company probably earns 2 to 3 times what they pay you, or let's say $100,000 on your efforts. That means you could usually double your salary if you did the same work as an independent consultant.

Let's look at the NBA again.

The Chicago Bulls owner crushes it. For example, he has made $55 million per season on average over the last five years. Those numbers are just nuts. Can you imagine making that much money for a year's worth of ownership? (Not work, *ownership*). Michael Jordan was an expert. He made a reported $100 million in his entire NBA career for his expertise in basketball. The other deals he inked from Nike are what made him most of his money.

**I want to address the skeptic in us all...**

By now we might encounter a skeptic, who might say, "Yeah ok, who has the money to buy an NBA team? I don't have money to buy a team like the Chicago Bulls." I promise you, true owners do not think that way. Instead of saying, "I can't afford the Chicago Bulls," they would ask, "How *can I* afford the Chicago Bulls?"

That question will likely break your brain. It sounds almost impossible at first. But with research and time you'd start to explore your imagination a little bit.

You would work your way up to owning a team by starting small and thinking like an owner now.

That's something you work up to.

If you made it your life mission to own a professional sports team, I bet you'd figure out a way.

And to the skeptics I'll say... your points are almost always valid... and yet there is almost always a path. You owe it to yourself to try. Great things are done by those of us who risk looking like fools to figure things out.

**Here's a concrete example of the "How can I afford it?" question.**

We are not taught the value of ownership, the safety of ownership, or the wealth of ownership. If you have a dream to be an expert at something, to play basketball, dance, or sing, please do that for yourself.

I'm sharing this with you to illustrate the potency of ownership. I believe if you were taught the skills of ownership for 15 years of your life instead of how to be an employee, you'd be more comfortable being an owner. Owners are in the background. You don't see them on TV like experts. They are the guys printing most of the money. Their income is not at risk if they don't show up, and they focus on the skills of ownership.

Let me make this concrete. There is a very popular four-story commercial building in downtown Des Moines, Iowa. It is an envy downtown. It is fully rented and has six tenants paying rent to the owner. Most real estate investors in Des Moines want it.

I happen to know the owner. He was my college professor.

Back in 2006, it was for sale for $1.6 million, and he bought it without using any of his own money.

Here's how.

He first asked the question, "How can I afford it?"

With that question in mind, he applied for an Historic Tax Credit. That means he would maintain the historic look as best he could so he could get tax credits from the government. When he applied he got $1 million in tax credits.

What that means is that he would not have to pay taxes on one million dollars of income. That's dope. Liquid gold. Real estate is nuts.

Next, he went online to Google to find people who would buy these tax credits for cash. There are very wealthy people who pay a lot in taxes, and these people buy tax credits to save money. He found and sold one million in tax credits to a guy for $900,000. This means the guy paid him $900,000 and instantly saved $100,000 on his taxable income. That's an instant 10% return on your money.

And my professor got $900,000 in cash, for a $1.6 million building.

Next, he had to hire renovators, so he used the rest of the money on a down payment for the construction loan. My professor was also a real estate agent, so he took the $70,000 commission he made and used that for the down payment as well.

Today, that building is worth over $6 million on the county assessor site. And it's been fully rented and cash flowing since day one.

He will probably sell it someday and easily make over $5 million in profit.

He is the owner. He didn't use his own money. And anyone with the proper knowledge could have pulled off that deal.

With stories like these, why do people choose to be an employee? Because of years of conditioning and programming telling us that being an owner is riskier than being an employee.

No. Being unknowledgeable is risky.

Just one deal like this could setup a family for life.

Let me share a little more about how I approach ownership.

I like to set up businesses (in the beginning) with the ability to walk away from them. From the very beginning, I make sure the business income is not dependent on my time or expertise. Most people get into business to be the expert. I do not. I get into business to be the owner. It's a very different way of life.

It requires humility (and a different kind of intelligence). It requires trust in others because I have to hire people. It requires sales skills to deliver the vision I have. Outsourcing skills. And it requires resourcefulness to put together lucrative deals for everyone.

When I started out, I thought of finding problems, selling solutions, growing revenue to $100,000 or so, then passing it off to someone I trust to run. I usually keep 80% or more of the business if I'm involved in the starting process, up to $100,000 in revenue. If I don't start it, I'll give more to the team.

When I step away, I take 25% of the profits for each business and invest the rest into the CEO and the team to run it. If I'm actively working in the business, I like to pay myself 50% of the profits from the business.

Now, I am experimenting with getting ideas and teams together and sharing more equity. I currently have two badass CEOs who I love dearly; they run the businesses while I stay in my zone of creation and singing if I feel like it. We are all in our zones of genius.

The skill of ownership and how to hire CEOs and structure deals can be a pretty in-depth topic, but I keep that stuff simple. For now, just think of ownership as this list of criteria.

1. Does the business income depend on my time? (Am I building something I can step away from?)
2. Do I have to be the expert for the business to succeed?

3.  Do I have the key metrics in place I can track to ensure the business is operating well? (25% minimum profit margins if I've stepped away, 50% if I'm actively working on it.)

Starting a business when you're not the expert is nerve-racking for many people. They wonder how in the world they could possibly add value when they aren't the one with all the knowledge.

"Won't someone take the idea?"

"What would my role be?"

"How could I pull this all off?"

Those questions should become clear as you download this book to your brain. If you can make the leap to ownership by using this book, you'll be richly rewarded for it with epic freedom.

If you can't yet tell, I am very passionate about this topic. Being an owner can set up generations of wealth for your family if you do it right.

## Exercise for Building Owners Thinking

Start by recognizing that you don't want to be the expert anymore. You want to be an expert at putting experts in place. The next chapter will help you build ownership thinking by being the newbie, not the expert.

# CHAPTER 16:

# BECOME A NEWBIE

Once I spent a month at a monastery hanging out with some monks. You know, trying to find peace and stuff. The monks were awesome. These monks were more modern than I had pictured when I arrived. They weren't the "money is evil" monks. They were still interested in understanding the skills required to make money so they could do good with it.

One day, when they were talking about raising funds for their monastery, the head monk knew of my track record and asked if I could help. I threw on a big old smile, "Would you like me to teach you how to create money from thin air?"

They said yes.

I had the monks (seven in total) sit in a circle and showed them how to cold call yoga studios to ask them about their most consistent problems. I cold called a couple of times myself to give them the script and then turned them loose. They all took turns watching each other. It was hilarious to see all the feelings and nerves that came up for them.

*Ring, ring...*

Yoga studio: "Hello?"

Monk: "Uh...yeah... Hi... So... Hey there... So..." [He pauses and grumbles... feels slightly humiliated...while we all smile and watch. The monk collects his composure and continues.] "I'm working on an idea for yoga studios, but I'm not sure if it's a good idea or not, so I was wondering if I could run it by you to get your gut reaction?"

Yoga Studio: "Um...yeah... Sure, go ahead."

Monk: "I want to write a little report for yoga studios to solve their greatest challenges and help make them more profitable. Do you think that would be a report you'd ever want to read?"

Yoga Studio: "Oh...uh...yeah... I have a yoga class starting in a moment, but please tell me more. That would be very interesting."

Monk: "Well, that's wonderful. I can send you a copy when it's ready. Do you think you could help with my research and tell me what your top pains are? The things you wish you could just give up or have handled?"

Yoga Studio: "We have problems with... (each studio owner shared a list of similar problems)"

Monk: "Thank you. Would you like me to let you know when the report would be ready?"

Yoga Studio: "Yes, please. Here is my email."

One thing to note, the studio owner stayed on the call and was late to their own class to hear what the monk had to say. And the other interesting thing is that not one yoga studio rejected us. Not one. I think it's because the opening line is perfect.

Even if you already have a product to sell, you should use this as the opening line.

We heard yoga studios struggle with things like:

- Getting new students to come back after the first class;

- Properly hiring and managing work-share employees (turns out many studios allow students to attend classes for free in exchange for working there—lots of potential to create a system, guide, or software here);
- Following up with all customers on a regular basis;
- Filling every class.

Now, armed with these problems, we must find people who have the answers. The next step is to find the most successful yoga studios in the country and learn how they solve these problems. The way you find the best studios is pretty straightforward—find those who are highly rated with the most positive reviews on Google.

You can contact them and ask them if they'd like to be featured in a book by sharing their wisdom and tell them they can get the book for free when it's released by doing so—that way they'll get to see what other studios have said as well.

Here's an example email you could send:

Subject: Can we feature you?

Hello, your yoga studio looks excellent online, and that's why we are writing to you.

Would you like to be featured in our upcoming book: *Yoga Money: How Studios Maintain Excellent Profits*?

We are writing a guide on how yoga studios maintain profitability, and we really liked what you are doing and your online reputation. It looks like you have it together from what we see online.

We were wondering if you'd like to be featured in this upcoming book by sharing what you do to maintain a successful studio? For your participation, we will give the book to you free when it's ready and promote your studio in the book!

If you're interested, we just need to conduct a phone interview with you.

We would turn the phone interview into a transcript, then show that to you for verification of course.

Reply back and let us know if you have any questions, and we can chat further,

—

Dane

Something to note about the email and the title of the book. This is a great topic for yoga because money is generally a struggle for spiritually inclined industries. So this book is strategically named because of what yoga studios struggle with.

I think almost any studio owner would be interested in this book.

**This is how you become the newbie.**

This is the skill of facilitation. No product. No idea. Just understanding how to add value and bring information together. Note: We never took it to this step because the monks were more interested in learning the process than completing this particular business.

Can you see how much potential is available to you if you humble yourself and become a beginner? You start by asking questions. You don't have to be great when you start. You can facilitate while being a complete newbie.

Then you own the outcome.

Now, I hope you use a little creativity here; otherwise, we might have hundreds of yoga profitability guides out there. But that might not be a bad thing.

Yoga needs to stay around, ya know?

The meta-pattern for being a newbie looks like this:

1. Find an industry.
2. Find their biggest challenges.
3. Find an expert that knows how to solve it.
4. Bring the two together.
5. Charge money for value added.
6. Give that value for free to the experts providing it.

## Exercise for Learning to Be the Newbie

Find someone who has a problem that you don't know how to solve. Then, go find some information that would help them, and send it over. Do it for free. Do some good. Facilitate. You'll see how the process goes and gain confidence.

# CHAPTER 17:

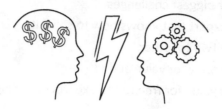

# OUTCOME THINKING VS.
# PROCESS THINKING

This skill is great because it shows you what to work hard at, so you can be lazy with the other things if you want.

Here's the core idea of this skill: one hundred processes could each achieve the same outcome.

So would you rather try and master one hundred different processes or focus on the core outcome you're looking to achieve, while experimenting with the process to see what fits? First-timers usually get stuck in the process, while the more experienced stay committed to the outcome.

The beginner who ignores outcome thinking will get slaughtered. The beginner who uses outcome thinking has a much better chance.

Tell me which of these two thoughts you'd like to start believing:

*How can I ever start a business if I work a job?*

*vs.*

*I know it's possible to start a business. I want one, and I'll figure out a way.*

Which one gives you more gasoline for the engine? If copywriting is Thor's hammer in business, outcome thinking is what you focus on smashing with the hammer.

Outcome thinking is a goal, but it is used differently and much more frequently. You write down a goal, but maybe you lose sight of it while you get stuck in the process. With outcome thinking, you revisit the outcome you want whenever you are stuck.

"What's the outcome we want here?" It becomes the guiding question every time you need to take action.

This is a huge advantage to being overwhelmed. If you are not clear about the outcome you want, then you will become easily defeated and over-whelmed. There are so many decisions to be made. Fatigue can set in if you're not clear on your desired outcome.

When my team and I create webinars to sell our programs, we create much better presentations when we check each slide and bullet against the question, "Is this section serving our outcome of inspiring an attendee to purchase our program?" This is how you develop presentations and missions with laser focus. Align all things to the outcome.

The outcome of this book is: someone reads it and successfully starts a business.

So, does each chapter, paragraph, and sentence aid that outcome?

If you're just getting started, you might set an outcome in two areas:

- I want to generate $10,000 per month.
- I want to set up a business with enough automation that I can run in two hours a day.

With those two outcomes in mind, you might land on some form of an automated customer acquisition business for a niche industry. Let's say, chiropractors. So you set an outcome like this:

◆ I want to help chiropractors acquire at least one new patient a month.

I spoke to a chiropractor about this the last time I went in for an adjustment. I asked him how much he would pay for a new patient and how much he thinks other chiropractors would pay. He said that he would pay around 1/6th of his customer value. For him, the total customer value factored out to $600, so he would pay $99 per patient generated.

Based on that initial conversation, I would have to generate one hundred new customers a month for a network of chiropractors to earn my goal of $10,000 per month. A quick Google search shows that 35 million people see a chiropractor annually. That's around 100,000 people a day or three million per month! Do you think that you could figure out how to direct one hundred of those to a network of chiropractors and earn the $10,000?

With focus, yes, you could.

The applications of outcome thinking are endless. Write it out, put it in front of you ("What is the outcome?"), and watch the freedom fall into place.

Show me what outcome thinking you are coming up inside the community with at StartFromZero.com/Yes.

## Exercise For Building Outcome Thinking

Take a deep breath with me right now.

Stating an outcome can be scary because it takes you out of fantasy and into reality. Be brave. Try it out right now with something.

You could say, "I want a body I'm happy with."

Then every decision could be checked against that outcome until it's automatic. Will eating this cheesecake support my outcome of being happy with the body I have? If yes, eat it; it not, don't.

You'll start to see how it's all choice.

With outcome thinking, it's important to practice stating outcomes and seeing how they feel to you. Don't be afraid to change an outcome. Try on several until you find the one that really lands for you.

Think about the outcome you want while reading this book. Think about the outcome you want for the current projects you are working on. Start cutting away things that don't align and build in the things that do.

If you want to start a business and run it in two hours a day, can you compare that outcome to some of your behaviors and see if that behavior will support the outcome?

It's super clear, but few do it.

If you need a little extra help with outcome thinking, visit StartFromZero.com/Yes to get it a five-minute guided meditation with questions to help you clarify and get something written down.

# CHAPTER 18:

# INCOME HAPPINESS

What is income happiness?

Income happiness is money you don't have to work for.

You could call it passive income. But unless you're investing in stock dividends or other similar investments, passive income is an illusion.

A more accurate term is asset-based income.

**You want assets** that produce income with little on-going work. And it isn't lazy; it's just smart to do. That's how you get wealthy and stay income happy.

The kind of assets I'm talking about are business assets. And remember, a business is best described as...

Customer → Uses A Mechanism → To Get A Result

That's how you make good money.

Assets might sound scary or boring or intimidating, but they are simple and sexy. Love yourself an asset. An asset can be simple. It could be a single-page website selling background music for video editors, for example.

Something like...

Video editors are always on the lookout for good B-roll music. It's a pain for them. So once you talk to a video editor and make sure they'd buy this, you can hire out the mechanism to be built.

Remember, we focus on the customer and the end result they want, not fulfilling the mechanism.

You could find local musicians and pay them to record in the studio for a reasonable price. Find a DJ community online and ask around. Hire out a musician through a job board. Find a pianist in your town to play some music with an iPhone Voice Note, hit record, and call it a day (Hah, kidding. Kidding. Or am I? It all depends on what a video editor wants).

If I were to talk to a video editor, I'd adapt the five questions...

I'd start by saying... "I'm thinking of building a digital backing track product for video editors. Can I ask you some questions about that?"

1. What's your current problem, If any, with background music?
2. How do you go about getting background music now?
3. What happens when you don't find solid background music?

4.  If you could wave a magic wand, how would you solve this problem?
5.  What would you pay for that, if anything?

Then I'd ask them...

1.  What are your favorite products as a video editor?
2.  Where do you visit online to get good information?
3.  What online video editing communities do you hang out in?

Then once I have his favorite products, I can now target people on Facebook who like those products and advertise my backing track music. I can run ads where he visits online and see about running ads inside the community he visits or talk to other video editors there.

But now with those basics you'd have an asset, and with probably a week of research you'd know what to do.

Simple business. Simple page. Simple asset.

If you sold three of these per day, that would be $150 a day in asset income (minus expenses).

That's a $4,500-per-month asset, $54,000 per year. Let's say you spend $50 a day on ads to get those three sales. So you'd have $100 in profit, or around $36,500 per year take home.

But that's just one asset.

Income happiness is dope.

## Watch Me Have An Idea Extraction Conversation Live With A Video Editor Friend!

I was scared...

I felt the fear of talking to someone about this idea. So I faced it. It was scary and caused me hesitation and a racing mind. I reached out to a friend who was a video editor and asked him if he'd be down to have a recorded conversation for this book. I was afraid he'd say no. But he said yes. He was very excited to chat.

But it was vulnerable and scary for me to ask. And I did it anyway.

As I was having the conversation this profound realization dawned on me that business truly is not personal. We make it personal. Adding value and business in and of itself is not personal.

It's not personal if he doesn't like this idea. It's not personal if he does.

**It either works or it doesn't, it's either of interest to him or it isn't, and we make it personal with our own thoughts.**

This is the cardinal rule of successful entrepreneurship. We do not get to decide what works. We just listen.

I recorded a 27-minute conversation with this video editor as an example so you can see how I handled the conversation live. It was really fun. You can listen to it at StartFromZero.com/Yes.

With Income Happiness, here's what you want to remember.

**Every dollar you make is not equal.**

Here's how I got introduced to income happiness.

Back when I was 22, my life changed in a single moment as I overheard two Realtors having a conversation in another room.

I had just gotten my real estate license and was at my uncle's RE/MAX office. I was building my own website. I knew just enough to hack together something with Wordpress and was proud to be doing it.

Feelin' resourceful, ya know?

When I got lost, a Google search would fix it. I knew enough to be dangerous.

Back in that office, I was making my website and looking at a potential hosting platform to get it live. The hosting platform said that it would cost $8 per month for a Wordpress website and that I could host one thousand domains with just $8.

One thousand domains for $8 per month? Sheesh.

I was about to hit the purchase button...

Meanwhile, I heard a conversation taking place in the next room with two other Realtors.

> "Hey man, I hate my website. What do you use?"
> "Oh, dude, I love my website. I use the XYZ service."
> "Really? How much is it?"
> "$100 per month."

When I heard that number, my gut hit the floor, "What I rip off!" I thought to myself! "I'm only going to pay $8."

But what happened next blew me away.

The other Realtor said, "That's it?! I pay $200 a month for mine!"

At that point, I was thinking, "What the blazing H am I doing being a Realtor? This is lame. I'm going to sell agent websites instead."

Because that would be a real asset I could own instead of exchanging my time for money.

I did the math...

$8 per month expense.
100 Realtors paying me $100 a month.
$10,000 per month in monthly revenue.
For an $8 expense?

And the rest was history.

I never looked back.

P.S. It turned out my server cost me $200 to host 100 websites. So I guess my profit was just $9,800. Bummer.

But wait, I still had to get a product built.

Remember our basic business formula.

Customer → Uses A Mechanism → To Get A Result

The customer wants a result, and we need a mechanism to do it.

I had no idea how to provide 100 Realtors a website. So I hired out the mechanism and focused on the customer and results. The mechanism cost me $3,000 to build.

My first customer paid to fund 100% of the development, and then got the product free for life. So I built it for him and then I sold it to everyone else.

I was in business for next to nothing. I had income happiness and an asset.

Since then, I've slowly been building my equity and automating income. It seems I was fortunate to have zero tolerance for inefficient, un-automated income. Most people unfortunately look to what their skills are and use just those with little thought on how to efficiently generate income.

But with this book, you won't get stuck there.

Never forget, you are the only person responsible for your income happiness. Don't depend on someone else for your income happiness. Now go create it!

# CHAPTER 19:

# LEARN FROM MISTAKES & BREAKS OF INTEGRITY

I did something stupid and made a big mistake in my career.

I stole someone's work and used it as my own.

This is how I handled it and what I learned.

First I'll say it was also one of the most significant things that ever happened to me because of what I have chosen to learn from it and how I changed.

I want to tell you what I did because I don't want you to make the same mistake.

Here's what happened. When writing a marketing letter, you often look at examples to get inspiration. People collect these marketing examples and call them swipe files.

You can Google "weight loss swipe files" or "make money swipe files" and go down a rabbit hole.

Well, I found a great sales letter from a top expert to swipe. But I was stupid, careless, and lazy in what I borrowed and stole his work.

This expert found out and contacted me, telling me to take it down. When I got the email, I pulled down the letter in one business day and issued an apology a few days later.

But it hurt.

I lost a mentor, I lost a key employee who left that was critical, and the respect of a good friend as well.

The dust settled, and then, five years later, this expert decided to tell the world, and I was publicly bashed for it and called a scam.

So if you ever feel tempted to copy someone's work, take the time to believe in yourself and make something unique. The world needs more of what you have to say, not more of the same.

And this chapter is my official apology to Ramit Sethi, and everyone who was hurt or involved in that process. I will always be sorry for ruining a relationship with you and taking your work.

I also want to apologize to you, the reader, if I've let you down in some way by sharing this.

I want you to know that I have grown and changed, and this was a deeply embarrassing moment.

Judge me not by my mistakes but by how I handle them.

I stand in the truth and embarrassment of my mistake to let you know you are not your mistakes. That if you did something wrong, that it will be OK. I am still alive and still successful.

Learn from them so you do not repeat them.

You are accountable for your own actions, so if you screw up, own it, then learn and become better.

Do not shrink into your mistakes and disappear. The world needs you.

In my opinion, we are always worthy of another chance.

## Exercise to Build the Skill of Learning from Loss and Mistakes

It's rather simple. Take your greatest mistake and ask yourself what you have learned. Write yourself a letter about what you learned. Once you have the learning, you still stop remaking it. If you avoid learning the lesson, you will keep making it.

If you need to apologize and it is warranted, I'd recommend it. But don't expect forgiveness, apologize to apologize.

Ok, now that we got through that low point. Let's get back to the action!

# CHAPTER 20:

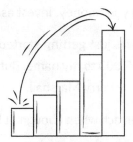

# HOW TO MAKE THE BIGGEST LEAPS

"Hey man," I said to a good friend.

"Would you think my lifestyle was possible unless you saw it firsthand?"

He thought for a moment...

I kept talking, "for example, if you didn't actually see me hanging out on the sofa on a Tuesday at 11:00 a.m., would you have known *this* is possible?"

He said, "No, I would not."

The difference between my friend and I was that I believed it was possible before I did it. He only believed it was possible after he saw it. So I lived the life of envy.

Because I like to believe things that others saw as impossible.

With that intention in mind, I took courses from really smart experts who promised big things and learned their business methods.

It changed my life rapidly.

And that's what this section is about.

Here's how I came to be the way I am.

Investing in myself has changed my life more rapidly than anything else did. Don't be stingy with your money. Invest as much as you safely can.

I'll never forget when I was just getting started in business, around the age of 24, I had maybe $5,000 to my name. But I spent $1,500 of it on a Google Adwords course by Perry Marshall.

It made me sick to my stomach when I bought it because I was so nervous.

But it changed my life because good courses can change your life.

Here's how mine changed with this particular course.

I went to Chicago for the closing seminar. I was extremely nervous. I had my nicest outfits. I got to sit around the table with a bunch of 40-year-old business people drinking and laughing about their adventures (who were not dressed nearly as sharp).

In between their drinks, one guy said, "Do you guys remember the days before CAN-SPAM? I used to buy and sell email addresses like a whore! Like a whore!"

Everyone laughed. Then the dust settled...

I asked, "How much did you make doing that?"
"$400,000 a year man."

Wow. I didn't know that ever existed. And while I'm not interested in doing such a thing that was probably responsible for CAN-SPAM forming, I like learning what's been done before because I take the good from every example I hear.

"What do you do now that you can't do that?"
"I own a press release service that helps people promote their brands; that does millions too."
"Oh really? How does that process work?"

And right from the horse's mouth I got one incredible example after another of people's businesses. I loved it so much.

It was an incredible evening. I loved getting to know this "odd" man.

These "odd" people became my friends. The random folks crushing it online. All because I bought a course.

**Then the next day I got to meet Perry.**

Perry came strolling in with a Hawiian shirt on and some swagger. The dude was nerdy, and I loved it.

I gulped and walked up to him when he came into the room and held out my hand. "Perry, it's so nice to meet you, I'm Dane."
"Nice to meet you, Dane."

My mind started racing, and I started talking to myself. "Oh crap it's Perry, he's talking to you now, keep it cool! Keep it cool!"

When I met him, I told him I had a recruiting software making me around $4,000 a month, and he looked at me and said...

"Great work. You must be proud."

I was stunned to hear those words. "What? Good job?" I had trouble parsing what he said.

I thought he was going to say, "That's alright, but you're not good enough yet kid."

But he didn't. He extended love and encouragement to me on something I worked very hard at.

And that moment changed my life.

Perry Marshall told me: "Great work." I thought I had achieved nothing up until that point with my $4,000 per month business. All the marketers online made me feel so small, talking about their million dollar launches and such. I thought I was a joke comparatively.

But Perry's words changed my attitude. They gave me a confidence I had never felt before. I went through maybe 25% of the course because that was all I needed. I thought I bought the course for the information, but it turns out I bought it for access to the creator, to shake his hand, and for the community.

That $1,500 turned into hundreds of thousands of dollars, just for the confidence boost.

I suddenly felt like I was important.

Fast forward to today, I have more money, and so I spend more on courses.

As I was writing this book, I spent $5,000 on a course by Alex Becker that teaches how to sell with YouTube ads. But I won't personally take this one myself. The real reason I bought that course was to get access to Alex and the Facebook group of other top marketers. Inside that group is where I met a 15-year-old who's deeply inspired me by hiring experts to teach courses he just sells.

A 15 year old is creating companies in there without being the expert on the subject matter.

And also, I bought the course for my team to take and implement. This is something you can do as you get more and more successful. I will buy the course, and then I pay someone to go through it and implement the content. That team member is usually very grateful to be learning something new.

It's a win win.

But please remember... I paid $5,000 mainly for the community because my brain changes when I'm around more successful people. I was ready to pay $10,000, but I got an early member price.

I need these connections to shape my brain to achieve the things that are important to me.

That $5,000 will likely be worth over one million dollars in the next three years.

I'm deeply sad to see how little people invest in themselves. How stingy people are to get help or buy courses. To that I say: Buy courses, buy programs, buy products, even if you don't finish them. You won't need to to get a return on your investment.

You usually only need one big idea from a course to get your value back.

Every course I buy changes my life because of the community. You get to be around other people who invest in themselves.

(Note if you buy a lot of courses and need help taking action, those are identity level issues and are solvable! We have the free guide to help with that at StartFromZero.com/Yes.)

But let me also stress that I will buy courses that I never take action on. I just want the knowledge. What ends up happening is years later it pours out of me in another way. I don't always take action on the courses I buy, and I'm OK with that.

Another day... I got the chance to meet a very successful marketer who was a legend to me when I was getting started. One day he took me up to his attic and showed me all the products, courses, and the books he had purchased.

He had shelves and shelves of thousand-dollar products.

"I went through each of these for about an hour each morning then implemented one thing that I learned each day."

Well, it showed.

Think about it. If he was investing in his learning for an hour each morning, and doing that for years, imagine the quantity of products he would have bought.

And this guy was a hero to me back when I was getting my start online. Thanks for showing me your attic, Tellman Knudson!

So in terms of developing this skill, ask yourself what you need most. Don't look for secrets because they are a waste of time. Look for what you need at a high level and seek out those who can help.

Be strict on all the things which don't provide you with a great return. Be open on all things that do. Don't buy shady stuff like "How to flip products on Ebay." Don't look for loopholes. Look to build your character and skill set. Get the reputable programs with track records and results and communities.

Get the programs that stop you from exchanging time for money.

And have fun making new friends.

# THE SEVEN-DAY ADVENTURE TO OPENING YOUR MONEY MIND

This following adventure you're about to embark on is the one thing I did that I tripled my income.

When an artist wants to learn how to paint, they might go to a museum and copy a piece of art to learn to paint like a master.

When the famous composer Bach wanted to learn music, he copied sheet music by hand in the evenings by moonlight.

When the late Dan Kennedy wanted to learn how to sell, he copied hundreds of sales letters that sold millions of dollars' of products, all by hand.

So when I wanted to learn how to sell, I did this for 90 days straight for one hour per day.

This is what tripled my income. Copying great sales letters by hand for one hour each day.

To my knowledge, the fastest and best way to acquaint yourself with building the skills for making money is to study the greatest money-making advertising letters of all time.

Here you will read one great advertisement per day for seven days. Just read one each day and look for the similarities. Pay attention to how they position the problem and then the product, and then pay special attention to how they ask for money. You want to model all of this.

These letters can be modeled in all kinds of industries if you find the deeper patterns in them. In general, you'd want to read as many ads as possible from John Carleton, Eugene Schwartz, Gary Halbert, or Dan Kennedy.

But here are the seven I recommend you read.
One per day.

Bonus points if you copy them by hand. But it takes longer to do that. Don't try to copy a letter in a day. Copy one by hand each week slowly. Going slow is what creates the progress.

You can conveniently find the seven sales letters at StartFromZero.com/ Yes or on Google.

Day 1: Read "The Wall Street Journal Sales Letter"
Day 2: Read "Burn Disease Out Of Your Body" by Eugene Schwartz
Day 3: Read "Do You Have The Courage to Earn $500,000 A Year?" by Eugene Schwartz
Day 4: Read "Cage Fighter Ad" by John Carleton
Day 5: Read "They Laughed When I Sat Down at the Piano" by John Caples
Day 6: Read "Beverly Hills Formula" by Gary Halbert
Day 7: Read "Million Dollar Smile Ad" by Gary Halbert

Again, I've got all of these in PDF form at StartFromZero.com/Yes, but you can also Google them.

And my friend Mike has a great resource of thousands of great advertising swipes at Swiped.co/StartFromZero.

Notice what happens to your mind as you get exposed to this kind of information. You'll start to see how you can powerfully ask for money and powerfully position a product.

You'll become a selling machine and a master of "sticky" communication.

# THE FOUR LEVELS OF ENTREPRENEURSHIP

This is an advanced section, written for those of you who want more complex information. In it, we have identified four growth stages an entrepreneur moves through.

I'm not going to be holding your hand here. Find what you need, then go and take action. If you harness this information, it will change the direction of your entire life.

No joke.

For example, one of the charts below contains an item labeled "Unconscious Humility." This is by far my favorite one. We all have an unconscious level of humility. This isn't the humility we show to the world; this is our secret, hidden, inner humility.

You can determine your level of unconscious (inner) humility by how willing you are to seek help.

I spoke to a business owner doing 10 million dollars per year. He told me this: "I realize I'm going to need help to get to where I want to go."

He was saying this to me while he was earning 10 million per year. Do you think this humble attitude helped him get there?

Absolutely. This distinction is life changing.

A beginner might be forever stuck because they have a lot of unconscious pride (they won't seek help or new information), whereas high-level entrepreneurs like Elon Musk consistently ask for help from others to make their visions come true.

This is the level of auto-pilot humility and behavior we operate from. You can just ask the following questions...

- How humble am I in how I behave?
- Am I OK asking for help?
- Am I OK outsourcing?

Humility requires vulnerability.

Take the time to explore your own unconscious (inner) humility and build it up. This one action alone could change how you live your life if you're willing to take the time to focus on it.

I believe that confidence is your birthright.
I created the charts below to help you identify and address your blind spots. This chart creates confidence.

We all have blind spots, and we all need help. **The brain is faulty if left to its own devices**. Here's how I want you to use this section:

1. Scan the charts below, line-by-line.
2. Find the line item that nails where you are currently.
3. Feel whatever emotions arise when you see something difficult to admit about yourself.
4. Identify the places where you are on the chart and then work on those aspects of yourself.
5. Turn up the self-compassion... Then go get more done.

If you fully digest this map, it will produce a magical and transformative effect for you.

It has for me.

I've broken the levels of entrepreneurship into four categories.

1.  Beginner
2.  Minor
3.  Major
4.  All Star

Have fun, and use this information below to fly in your life.

# Assess Your Level of Action & Results

First, let's look at the level of action and results you are currently getting by looking at the action map.

## How is your level of action?

|  | **Beginner** | **Minor League** | **Major League** | **All-Star** |
|---|---|---|---|---|
| **Action:** | Little | Inconsistent | Consistent | Leveraged |
| **Results:** | Low | Some | Great | Unlimited |
| **Freedom:** | Low | Low | Building | Unlimited |
| **Primary State:** | Driven by Survival | Often Stressed | Results Driven | Aligned Flow |
| **Potential Weakness:** | Lack of Desire | If They Focus on Personal Flaws | If They Lose Their Identity in Results | If They Lose the Vision |
| **Commitment:** | None | Weak | Strong | All In |

The biggest lever you can build for action and results is to get very clear on your commitment and go all in. You can do it gradually by building confidence and reading this book. Be gentle with yourself as you build this kind of confidence.

What does being "all in" look like? Who can we look to as an example?

If you want to see what being all in looks like in terms of the books you'd read, visit StartFromZero.com/Yes for that list.

Let's look at someone like Elon Musk and the actions he takes. He's moving humanity forward—he has "leveraged action" down. His results are in the category of "unlimited," and he's living in the state of "aligned flow." The dude is all the way in. If he loses, he loses big. If he wins, he wins big. He's not very good at being in the middle.

You don't have to be big like Elon Musk to be all in. You could have a much smaller desire than "sending a human to Mars" and still be all the way in. When your commitment becomes written by heart, and there is no turning back, you unlock an immense creative power.

> "Commitment is the ultimate assertion of human freedom. It releases all the energy you possess and enables you to take quantum leaps in creativity. When you set a one-pointed intention and absolutely refuse to allow obstacles to dissipate the focused quality of your attention, you engage the infinite organizing power of the universe."
>
> — Deepak Chopra

The immensity of fear that can come up when you think about being "all in" is primal. The concept of being "all in" could fill an entire second book. If you have issues with commitment, I think it stems more from a lack of trust in yourself than from a fear of failure.

Get help with commitment if you need it. There is no shame in it. Just like my 10-million-per-year-business friend from above.

For now, just know that being "all in" on your vision is what is needed for your action map to fly.

## How is your sales mindset?

Next, we look at your selling mindset. Where do you land here?

| | Beginner | Minor League | Major League | All-Star |
|---|---|---|---|---|
| **View Of Sales** | Negative | Afraid | Fun | Noble |
| **Salesmanship** | "I Don't Sell." | Sloppy (No Process) | Solid (Follow a Process) | Moves People to Action |
| **Crafting Offers** | No Offers to Craft | Chosen Ignorance | Confident | Expert |
| **Competition** | Fearful. Only One Idea is Allowed | Fearful. Obsessed With Competition | Ready. Many Competitors Allowed | Grateful for Competition |
| **Mindset** | Only One Idea Can Be Produced | Compete On Price | Compete On Results | Competes With Self |

Do you see selling as noble? Imagine you arrive on the lot of a car dealership:

> *Salesman*: So what brings you in today?
>
> *You*: I'm looking for a car for my family.
>
> *Salesman*: Ah, wonderful. Can you tell me what's most important to you in a car for your family?
>
> *You*: Safety.

*Salesman*: Safety, great. Is having a status symbol important to you in a car? Do you need a car to have a certain visual appeal?

*You*: Actually, that would be preferred. I don't want to feel old.

*Salesman*: Ah, you don't really want to be seen driving a minivan I take it?

*You*: Hah, right.

*Salesman*: OK, so safe, and some visual appeal in the car, a little status. That sounds wonderful. Is there anything else that is important to you in a car?

*You*: Yes, my wife has to like it.

*Salesman*: Hah, great! OK. So we've got safety, some visual appeal/ status, and your wife's seal of approval. Anything else?

*You*: No, show me what you got.

Do you see the salesman's purpose here? He has one directive: to match the customer's desire with the right product. He's not pushy, he's not manipulative, he's not tricky. He's listening, asking questions, and finding matches. And that, my friends, is why selling can be noble.

Because as a salesman with a noble intention you are directly helping someone get a perfect match.

If you don't think selling is noble, or that it even exists, you just haven't experienced it yet.

And one of my top students, Cris Urzua, can teach you how to sell with heart. I have a free interview with Cris at StartFromZero.com/Yes.

Let's look at another item in this chart. Competition. One of the biggest aha moments a new entrepreneur can have is that many ideas and competitors can still work.

Do you ever think, *Oh, that idea has already been done?*

If you believe only one idea or competitor is allowed, that's a big sign that you don't understand business yet.

By my estimations, Google was around the ninth search engine to be launched. They were number nine. You can have competition and still get started. Competition is usually a mirror showing us our own secret level of inadequacy at business.

If you fear competition, it's not the competition you actually fear. It's the fear of something else, and the competition is just waking you up to your own internal fears. Your fear actually has nothing to do with competition. It's with something else you'll need to explore.

Like not being good enough or capable enough.
The business world is far more abundant than most of us think.

Finally, let's look at the big list of personal skills that can really move the needle forward.

## How are your personal skills?

|  | Beginner | Minor League | Major League | All-Star |
|---|---|---|---|---|
| **Unconscious Humility** | Arrogance | Hidden Pride | "I'm the Best." | "I Need Help." |
| **View Of The World** | Luck & Chance | "I'm Missing Something." | Endless Possibilities | Here to Serve |
| **Self Identity** | What Others Say | How Others Respond | "I Get Results." | Steward to the Vision |
| **Confidence** | Low | False Bravado | High | Very High |
| **Emotions** | Lost | Fear/Anxiety | Excited | Pure Potential |

|              | Beginner | Minor League | Major League | All-Star |
|--------------|----------|--------------|--------------|----------|
| Intuition | Listens to Others | Fear-Based | Knowledge Based | Higher Vibration Based |
| Why | Unknown | Inauthentic | Self Based | Values Based |
| Focus | All Over | The Next Thing | Results | The Vision |
| Responsibility Taken | Blames Others | Blames Circumstance | High | Absolute Highest |
| Clarity Of Vision | No Vision | Fuzzy or Weak | Self Based Clear | Legacy Based Clear |
| Saying No | Can't Say | Hard Time | Decent | Comfortable |
| Level Of Fun | None | Mild | Strong | Inner Joy |
| When Discouraged | Become Paralyzed | Slows Down | Keeps Moving | Adjust With Data & Resets |
| Priorities | Do It Tomorrow | Comfortable Thing First | Highest Monetary Value First | Highest Values First |
| Negative Emotions | Run From | Blame Others | Try to Remove | Listen to |
| Personal Health | Toxic | Getting By | Vibrant | Exceptional |
| Personal Wealth | Possessions | Better Possessions | Achievement & Approval | From Being Itself |

Like I said at the beginning of this section, my favorite field here is "Unconscious Humility."

Can you imagine how much help Elon Musk needs to make his visions come to life? Can you imagine Elon Musk trying to start a business without getting help? This principle trickles down to the little things. Would you be able to hire someone to do your laundry? Would you be able to let someone help you with that?

It is OK to need help. It is OK to ask for help.

Unconscious humility is a game-changer. It could change your legacy.

I created a meditation to help you open up to asking for more help at StartFromZero.com/Yes.

If you took just one thing away from this entire section, deeply internalizing an unconscious level of humility would be my recommendation.

Another thing to note on this list is the skill of "intuition," which is internally directed guidance at the highest level of trust. I highly recommend developing your intuition.

You do, in fact, know what you need to do, right now in this moment.

## How to Upgrade

Upgrading is a very personal process. Go through the list above. Circle where you are at. If you are not at "all star" in the section, then place your hand on your heart and ask: "Hello heart that I love, how can I permanently change this for the better to become an all star?" The answer to this question will tell you where to focus your time and energy.

**This is an answer that you must discover for yourself.**

Often people will look at their chart results and say, "Great, now I see where I am; how do I get to the next section?" If you are looking for an answer, that shows a need to develop more personal leadership. And great leaders ask great questions, so you're already on your way there by asking the question.

The question is more important than the answer. And your intuition knows the answer, or knows how to find the answer.

For example, from the chart above, one of my friends was basing her identity on how others responded, instead of on her own values. She placed her hand on her heart and asked the question: "Hello heart that I love, how can I permanently change this identity issue for the better to move to the all star category?"

The heart's answer that came to her was simple. "Believe in yourself and keep doing the work. The identity issue will take care of itself." Nothing complicated. It's very simple.

> Go through the list above. Circle where you are currently.
>
> If you are not at "all star" in a particular section, then place your hand on your heart and ask... "Hello, heart that I love, how can I permanently shift this into all star for the better?"

## Becoming This Epic Vision

Visit this chart often. Check yourself against it. If you'd like to deeply embody these qualities, read the following section aloud until you have memorized it.

> I see commitment as a beautiful expression, as a way to know myself deeper, and I really want to know myself. I know that I may be afraid at times, but if I love myself more than fear, I will be safe to make decisions. I desire to create leveraged actions that ripple outwards and to have an unlimited sense of freedom through this commitment.
>
> Because I am starting to value these things, I will attract them into my life in surprising and new ways.

Selling is a noble act when done with heart. I realize much of sales seems to have ego, but I will have heart. I want to contribute to humanity by listening to the deep needs of others and matching those desires with complementary products. I see the primary role of a salesperson as not being a smooth talker but being a patient listener. I desire to enact the feeling of nobility within my mind and nervous system when I think of the word "sales," because of how I will serve others.

I will now recognize any hidden pride that I may have in certain areas, and I will surrender it and start asking for help from myself and others by trusting that I am always loved. I will see asking for help as a sign of powerful confidence with others, not weakness. I love it when people ask me for help, and I can see others will love it when I ask as well. I will create a powerful vision for myself and ask others to help me with it. I will source my sense of identity from how well I am using my naturally given talents and learn to say "no" when they do not align. I will pursue my highest value action first and learn from all negative feelings that arise, no matter how difficult.

I will do this because I deeply desire to see my potential before I die so I can love as many people as humanly possible and uplift the world with my life.

If you would like a full chart of this to print out or use as a desktop background, please visit StartFromZero.com/Yes.

# THE HALLS OF TRANSFORMATION

As an entrepreneur, you get to be yourself.

Not someone else.

It's important that you hear that.

You get to be yourself. In fact we flock around the world to learn from entrepreneurs who build businesses around themselves.

Please don't get into business to be someone else. Become an entrepreneur to be more of yourself. Entrepreneurship is a great place to do it. There are no limitations here.

In this section, you'll read about million-dollar businesses, six-figure businesses, and smaller players all crushing it in their own way. They all started from scratch using the framework you learned about in this book.

They were all students of mine and took the primary 6 month flagship course we offer at StartFromZero.com/Yes. They went through a grueling process and fundamentally transformed.

In each section you'll also see each entrepreneur's Hexaco personality traits! This is pretty ridiculous data.

It took me seven years to become a millionaire, and my top students did it in four years because of the knowledge I passed down.

In this section, I'm sharing stories of some of the students who have experienced the greatest transformations. My hope is that they will inspire you to stay true to yourself.

Maybe you'll build your business slower—maybe even faster. Maybe you won't make it to a million in revenue, but who cares? You'll see in these stories that what matters is that you're happy.

Let's get to work.

## Dave Rogenmoser:

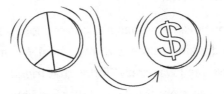

# ALMOST A MISSIONARY TO MILLIONAIRE

"I am happiest when I am creating something, not being an employee." —Dave

Dave had a big transformational journey...

He told me, "I used to believe money was bad and that people who had it were probably greedy. Now, I see money can be a tool for good, and money is the result of value created."

**Money is the result of value created, and It can be a tool for good.**

That is such a powerful belief. Try it on. Dave was stuck waiting for the perfect idea... "I was waiting until I found a good idea before I got started in entrepreneurship... But now I know there are millions of good ideas all around me, just waiting for someone to understand them and take action."

Can you imagine being in Dave's brain and seeing the world in the same way? Dave knows there are millions of good ideas around him every day, just waiting for someone to understand them and take action.

Believing this idea takes a powerful transformation of your way of thinking. The land of ideas is where most of us get stuck—waiting for that golden idea or trying to pick from the list you have. But it's only the place you get stuck if you stay uneducated.

Today, Dave owns a seven-figure software business, and he still doesn't even know how to program.

His transformation began years ago at a coffee shop. "I bought Start From Zero while I was drinking coffee with my friend. My friend was making fun of me and told me I was crazy. Today that friend is still in the same place, and I now own a multi-million dollar SaaS business, and I live in Austin with my beautiful family."

Before his transformation moment, he told me, "I wanted to be a missionary in India for the rest of my life, which would have been a beautiful path as well."

Dave jumped right in and started four different businesses over four years. Then he stumbled across his latest gem. Dave had been building his entrepreneurial brain for a while, when one day he browsing vacation packages on TripAdvisor and saw a notification saying, "Judy from Minneapolis booked this trip three minutes ago," and he had an aha moment.

He noticed that the notification made him want to purchase the trip. And then he thought, *I could make social proof notifications like this for other websites.*

He managed his risk... He followed Start From Zero framework of selling his idea before he built it to reduce the risk. Dave ran a webinar for his potential customers called "How to Increase Your Sales" and sold 40 people the $1,000 package for his potential tool. He essentially sold one year of the service upfront for $1000: 40 people at $1,000. So he made $40,000 to build the product, then he got to work building his product.

Where's the risk here? His risk is purely the rejection of an idea. He hasn't risked building anything. He hasn't risked any money. He and his family are perfectly safe in this process.

After the successful webinar, Dave created UseProof.com—a social proof notification tool for purchase behavior to increase sales conversion. Today his business brings in millions of dollars.

But be careful here... Don't compare yourself to Dave now if you're just starting out. UseProof was Dave's fifth business. He got to practice on four other ideas. He was already successful in other business endeavors at this point—and had spent time building his brain so that when the idea hit, he knew what to do with it.

By taking time to build the structures in your brain, you know what to do with an idea. You don't wait for the idea.

Dave is now a CEO. He went from wanting to be a missionary and having the employee mind to being a SaaS CEO. It's pretty amazing. But this is truly what's possible.

What's it like to be a CEO? Dave used to think, *Being a CEO and running a company means everyone would work for me and serve my interests.* Now, he says, "I've learned that being a CEO feels a lot like working for everyone else on my team and keeping them happy, motivated, and aligned."

Let's break down Dave's latest business.

### Who's the customer?
Small and medium-sized businesses selling anything on their websites.

### What's their pain?
They can't convert enough of their traffic into sales and don't have the skills to change that.

### What's your solution?
UseProof.com

Dave shows live social proof notifications on their site that show recent customer activity, like purchases or sign-ups. "Dane from San Diego just bought this course 2 minutes ago." When visitors see these notifications, they are about 10 to 15% more likely to take the same action.

**What's your offer?**
$29 per month on the low end.
$999 per month on the high end.

Dave is just a human being like the rest of us. Dave had the same fears we all do when starting... He told me, "I was afraid I would fail and everyone I told about the business would think I was a loser."

**I asked him how many times he thought of giving up, and he told me...**

"Probably once a week I considered throwing in the towel, though at the same time I never REALLY considered it. I've always just kept putting one foot in front of the other and my co-founders help me."

When I asked what his "why" was, he told me... "I want to create a business that can provide shelter (financial, fun, etc.) for all my friends and family and be a vehicle for impacting others in the world."

# Dave's three tips:

1.  Optimize for quick learning, not for success. Fail as fast as you can over and over and over again and get really comfortable failing. Make a game of it. You'll learn so much faster than everyone else and start to have a different relationship with failure that will become a superpower.

2.  Spot problems and start to build mental frameworks for creating solutions. Probably a year into entrepreneurship, I would just walk down the street and practice spotting problems and fixing them. "That grocery store looks like it's getting low foot traffic. Here are

three ideas I have for how they could increase that." "This street has so many potholes. Here's an idea for how to create and monetize a pothole filling company."

3. Start immediately, or before you know it, you'll have more expenses, a family, and a home, and your willingness to take risks will be much lower. Wherever you are, start right now. It'll never get easier.

## Dave Roganmoser's Hexaco Score:

| Category | The Score (0 to 5) | Median Score (0 to 5) |
|---|---|---|
| **Honesty-Humility** | 2.44 | 3.22 |
| Sincerity | 2.50 | 3.25 |
| Fairness | 1.75 | 3.38 |
| Greed-Avoidance | 1.25 | 2.63 |
| Modesty | 4.25 | 3.63 |
| **Emotionality** | 1.94 | 3.34 |
| Fearfulness | 1.25 | 3.00 |
| Anxiety | 1.75 | 3.75 |
| Dependence | 3.00 | 3.25 |
| Sentimentality | 1.75 | 3.50 |
| **eXtraversion** | 4.38 | 3.50 |
| Social Self-Esteem | 5.00 | 4.00 |
| Social Boldness | 4.50 | 3.13 |
| Sociability | 3.50 | 3.63 |
| Liveliness | 4.50 | 3.63 |
| **Agreeableness** | 3.94 | 3.00 |
| Forgivingness | 5.00 | 2.75 |
| Gentleness | 2.56 | 3.25 |
| Flexibility | 3.50 | 2.75 |

| Category | The Score (0 to 5) | Median Score (0 to 5) |
|---|---|---|
| Patience | 5.00 | 3.25 |
| Conscientiousness | 2.56 | 3.47 |
| Organization | 1.75 | 3.38 |
| Diligence | 5.00 | 3.88 |
| Perfectionism | 1.00 | 3.63 |
| Prudence | 2.50 | 3.25 |
| Openness to Experience | 3.81 | 3.31 |
| Aesthetic Appreciation | 2.50 | 3.25 |
| Inquisitiveness | 4.25 | 3.13 |
| Creativity | 3.75 | 3.63 |
| Unconventionality | 4.75 | 3.38 |
| Altruism | 4.50 | 3.38 |

# 50 HOUR WORK WEEKS TO TRAVELING THE WORLD WITH A LAPTOP

"I've always believed deep down that I was made for great things, but no one had given me the opportunity to prove it. Then I realized it's nobody else's job to give me an opportunity; I've got to take it for myself. My deepest "why" is to not have to work after age 40 so that I can be 100% devoted to being a great father and a great husband, which will be my greatest project in life."
                                                                    — Steve

What happens if you truly commit? As I said, it's not only about the result or the lifestyle. It's about the transformation; it's about who you become.

Let me show you what I mean and why it's really about the transformation more than the result.

**This is how Steve used to live and think:**
"I'd sleep as late as humanly possible, wake up in a rush, fight traffic, get to work, waste as much time as possible, half-ass work, and daydream about a better life while doing nothing to get there. I'd complain to others about work and take almost no responsibility for myself or my decisions.

I'd smoke a lot of weed and then feel guilty about it. I'd eat junk, avoid exercise, and neglect my relationship."

**This is how Steve lives now:**
"Now, I meditate and do fitness first. I journal in my daily planner, then in my gratitude journal. I work three solid hours on my most creative task. I practice guitar, play piano, or work on a short story or screenplay. I travel regularly. I enjoy my city. I read in the evenings. I enjoy evenings with a few close friends. I'm generous with my time and money and help others when they need it."

Many of us mistakenly think that if we pursue our dream, it is selfish. But you can see here that when you put yourself first as Steve did, it's actually generous and not selfish because he has so much more to give to the world.

Steve busted his tail learning how to build a software as a service business, and in the process of learning this business model, he acquired powerful skills and fell in love with copywriting.

He used to work 10 hours a day in addition to a commute, tied down to one city. No wonder he was smoking pot. That would have sucked. Today he works three to four hours a day with no commute. He lives in exotic locations, and he earns $15,000 to $20,000 per month as a copywriter.

How long did it take for him to make these numbers happen? Just four years.

**But he's completely free. Now he is set for the rest of his life.**
Steve had some pretty crippling beliefs preventing entrepreneurship. Here's what he used to believe.

"I have zero valuable skills in business. I don't know how to negotiate or sell. I already have enough in life, and I should be happy with what I have. I shouldn't ask for more and just take what I've got. I'm too old at 29 and should be getting married, getting a mortgage, and thinking about kids and family."

Now with a little help, he has shifted to some powerful beliefs. Here's what he had to say:

> "I can have any skill set I want provided that I have the desire to dedicate time to mastering it. Making millions of dollars does not correlate to the lifestyle I want. Making $250,000 a year as a solopreneur is a fucking amazing life. I have value that no one can touch except me. I have a skill set no one can take away from me. My relationship with money is completely different. My favorite thing about money is that I can always make more of it. I have a net worth now and financial security, which does wonders for my anxiety. I'm young, and now that I know how much can be done in four years, there's really no age limit on anything. On top of building two businesses in four years and 5x-ing my Income, I've also learned two languages, moved to a new country, bought property, learned piano, been on more than one hundred dates in different languages, and fallen in love with someone I feel I deserve."

As I said, it's about the transformation.

**Let's look at Steve's business model that makes it all happen.**

Remember, the business isn't what's critical for the success; it's the transformation of the person behind the business you want to look at. Steve could make any business he wanted now. However, learning business examples does wonders for the brain in terms of showing what's possible.

So, here's his business breakdown using our four-part framework. Who's the customer? What's the pain? What's the solution? What's the offer?

**Who's the customer?**
Steve: Large alternative health and supplement companies with several products across several sub-niches.
Pretty specific customer, yeah?

**What's their pain?**

Steve: Finding reliable writers that hit deadlines and communicate well. There are three things for copywriters to do: convert, deliver on time, and communicate with clients. A successful copywriter needs to do two out of three of those things. Converting is obviously important, but surprisingly the biggest pain point with these clients are flakey writers who miss deadlines and avoid communication.

**What's the solution?**

Steve: The solution is usually long-form sales letters, email campaigns, and video sales letters for selling products. I talk to clients when they expect me to, and I over-communicate. I am religiously strict about hitting deadlines and being honest with clients about setting them. I submit quality, error-free work on time, without fail. If a deadline is missed and not communicated, I refund 10% of the monthly invoice.

**What's the offer?**

Steve: Depending on the client, my monthly retainer rates are between $7,500 and $10,000 a month. One-off project rates are between $6,000 and $12,000, depending on scope and duration. Retainer work comes with unlimited edits and full access to my calendar for calls but with a clear understanding of boundaries. For the bigger clients, I'll charge $10,000 for a sales letter package plus 3% of backend sales.

**This is what Steve shares on his timeline to success.**

"Year one was a disaster, and in year two, things got steadily above $3,000 to $5,000 a month. Year three moved to a steady income of above $5,000 a month, and year four bumped up to $10,000+ per month. I have been at $15,000 to $20,000 a month for many months now."

This is important; you can't fake the skills to make money. There isn't anything you "get away with." There are firm skills you need that spit out the cash. It's just about learning those skills along with a transformation of who you are.

Steve had two other failed business attempts and one half-attempt to invest and open a restaurant.

When asked about his greatest fear, he said, "I fear I have no value, no skills, no one will take me seriously, I will be shamed in front of everyone I know, and they'll all be proven right that I made all the wrong decisions."

I've included Steve Erl as a story here because of the importance of learning entrepreneurial skills instead of quick fixes. Steve pursued building a business and found what he loved in the process, copywriting. He had the courage to stick with what he loves, instead of trying to build a business and wear the other hats. I think it's a bold move. He's a great leader in his own life, has the core skills of an entrepreneur, and can use them however he now sees fit.

## Steve's three tips:

1.  Don't ever do things based on someone else's perception of suc-cess. Stop looking for everyone's approval. Don't go to university because you don't have a real plan. Know yourself.

2.  Think clearly about what you want your life to look like day-to-day. Find someone who is living that life. Pay them for mentorship. Don't deviate from their advice. Master a valuable skill that is in demand.

3.  Make sure your money goals are in sync with your lifestyle goals. "Making a million dollars per year" is a tempting target, but "making $300,000 a year" is wayyyy easier and requires much less work and less stress and is a better fit for me and the life I want to live.

# Steve Erl's Hexaco Score:

| Category | The Score (0 to 5) | Median Score (0 to 5) |
| --- | --- | --- |
| Honesty-Humility | 3.00 | 3.22 |
| Sincerity | 3.50 | 3.25 |
| Fairness | 2.25 | 3.38 |
| Greed-Avoidance | 2.50 | 2.63 |
| Modesty | 3.75 | 3.63 |
| Emotionality | 3.81 | 3.34 |
| Fearfulness | 2.75 | 3.00 |
| Anxiety | 4.75 | 3.75 |
| Dependence | 4.00 | 3.25 |
| Sentimentality | 3.75 | 3.50 |
| eXtraversion | 3.38 | 3.50 |
| Social Self-Esteem | 3.75 | 4.00 |
| Social Boldness | 2.50 | 3.13 |
| Sociability | 3.00 | 3.63 |
| Liveliness | 4.25 | 3.63 |
| Agreeableness | 3.19 | 3.00 |
| Forgivingness | 3.50 | 2.75 |
| Gentleness | 4.00 | 3.25 |
| Flexibility | 2.75 | 2.75 |
| Patience | 2.50 | 2.50 |
| Conscientiousness | 4.00 | 3.47 |
| Organization | 4.75 | 3.38 |
| Diligence | 4.00 | 3.88 |
| Perfectionism | 3.75 | 3.63 |
| Prudence | 3.50 | 3.25 |
| Openness to Experience | 4.69 | 3.31 |
| Aesthetic Appreciation | 4.50 | 3.25 |

| Category | The Score (0 to 5) | Median Score (0 to 5) |
|----------|--------------------|-----------------------|
| Inquisitiveness | 4.50 | 3.13 |
| Creativity | 5.00 | 3.63 |
| Unconventionality | 4.75 | 3.38 |
| Altruism | 4.75 | 3.88 |

Fabi Mersan:

# NOW WORKS AT HOME WITH THE FAMILY CLOSE BY

---

"My 'why' is to have the freedom I want to be a present mother and wife. I want to empower and show women they can be more than just a mother and a partner. I want women to feel independent." — Fabi

Fabi lives in the warm climate of Paraguay with her husband and two children. She's always been determined no matter what she is working on. Tennis was her first devotion, and she learned her discipline skills there. As an example of her commitment, she'd often practice tennis three times a day and cycle through three pairs of workout clothes in a 24-hour period. Clearly, she's not afraid to put in the work.

People often ask me about the chance of success if they start. Often those people are not the ones who are successful. They come in with doubt. The ones who really shine come in gunning for the finish without a thought of anything else. Others who come in with doubt, but then handle it, get there as well. It's best to set your sights on the finish and not think of anything else. The greatest predictors of success are working hard and understanding commitment. If you try entrepreneurship but haven't built success in another area, or don't come in with successful qualities, you'll have to build those.

Fabi had wanted to be an entrepreneur from an early age. But, after graduating from college, she got a job and lasted only six months because she hated the work. She used the money from her job to pay for Start From Zero.

Now, she says, "I work four to five hours a day, tops."
And she did all this before turning 26.

## Here is Fabi's transformation:

"In the past, I believed I would never be successful because I have zero experience. I was afraid of being seen as a fraud and was very scared of failing."

"Now I see that success is not determined by the level of experience I have. I can achieve anything I want as long as I do it with commitment and passion. As long as I am transparent, things will be great. My authenticity is my biggest ally."

It was an adventurous road for Fabi. She tried five different business ideas until she landed on her current one. She thought of giving up countless times. "There are days where I think how easy it would be just to collect a paycheck, but I will never give up. My entrepreneurial spirit won't let me."

Note: Fabi tried five ideas and kept going. Many people try to succeed on the first idea. Sure, it can happen! But think of your first idea as the training to build your confidence. Let yourself be messy and just start.

Fabi started out in the physical therapy space, found a number of ideas, and even pre-sold a solution. She cut her teeth for a while with four ideas, building those entrepreneurial skills, until she noticed her own interest in helping women In Paraguay.

She created a community of female entrepreneurs in Paraguay to get to know her market in person. That makes a big difference. She did idea extraction in person through monthly meetups.

Over the year, she tested different courses with the ultimate idea of launching her own info product. She launched a course teaching women how to create blogs and found out they needed help with personal branding. She was surprised by this because she thought they would need help with marketing. But personal branding was the big pain. So Fabi went for it and got a postgraduate degree in personal branding in order to gain knowledge and create her own methodology. She created her method, validated it with one real client, and with all the lessons learned. Then she created and launched her 12-week intensive program.

She planned an in-person event in only 10 days, closed 25% of her audience into her program, and is now planning to expand events to Mexico.

Fabi joined Start From Zero in 2015 and took two years to start running her own business. In 2017, she earned $40,000, in 2018 she earned $60,000, and in 2019 she earned $120,000. And these dollar amounts are larger in Paraguay, where five US dollars can get you three cappuccinos instead of one in America.

Fabi says, "I found personal branding to be the perfect vehicle for my 'why' of helping women shine and become independent."

Let's break down Fabi's business into our customer, pain, solution, and offer framework.

### Who's the customer?
Service-based female entrepreneurs that want to launch their businesses but don't know where to even start or how to scale.

### What's their pain?
They lack clarity on what to do and how to do it. They know a lot about their industry but nothing about business and marketing, and they don't know how to structure the business.

### What's the solution?

FabiMersan.com

An in-person event on the basics of personal branding. Also, a twelve-week personal branding intensive to launch their own brand step-by-step.

**What's the offer?**
Event: $70 for a four-hour in-person event with Fabi. Then she sells her course at the end.

Her twelve-week intensive course breaks down like this:

- $497: Access to course, community, and email support.
- $897: Same as above plus online group meetings with Fabi.
- $1,297: Same as above plus three one-on-one sessions with Fabi.
- $2,500: one-on-one package. Doesn't sell this publicly, but for people who ask, she offers this package.

Fabi is a unique example because she's the only student living and working down in Paraguay as a stay-at-home mother. Your business can look however you want it too.

## Fabi's four tips:

1. Be patient; it's a process. Learn from others, take what you like and what works, and then at the end of the day, do you. Being authentic will get you further than any other strategy.

2. Understand your vision, understand your interests, understand your talents, then get to know the market you want to serve. Ask, ask, ask. Listen, listen, listen. (Note: Fabi could have gone with her gut, which was to sell marketing, but her customers wanted personal branding, so she listened.)

3. Self-confidence is the biggest issue I see. People don't take the time to get to know themselves, so they get lost in other personas they follow and admire, and that is where it becomes competition and you feel worthless, like you are never going to make it.

4.  I believe if people are sure about themselves, what they are worth, and where they want to go, everything will flow better. At least that's what I experience and what I see in my clients.

## Fabi Mersan's Hexaco Score:

| Category | The Score (0 to 5) | Median Score (0 to 5) |
| --- | --- | --- |
| Honesty-Humility | 4.13 | 3.22 |
| Sincerity | 4.75 | 3.25 |
| Fairness | 5.00 | 3.38 |
| Greed-Avoidance | 3.00 | 2.63 |
| Modesty | 3.75 | 3.63 |
| Emotionality | 3.25 | 3.34 |
| Fearfulness | 3.00 | 3.00 |
| Anxiety | 2.75 | 3.75 |
| Dependence | 3.50 | 3.25 |
| Sentimentality | 3.75 | 3.50 |
| eXtraversion | 3.38 | 3.50 |
| Social Self-Esteem | 4.75 | 4.00 |
| Social Boldness | 4.75 | 3.13 |
| Sociability | 2.25 | 3.63 |
| Liveliness | 3.00 | 3.63 |
| Agreeableness | 3.50 | 3.00 |
| Forgivingness | 3.50 | 2.75 |
| Gentleness | 3.50 | 3.25 |
| Flexibility | 3.50 | 2.75 |
| Patience | 3.50 | 3.25 |
| Conscientiousness | 3.81 | 3.47 |
| Organization | 4.00 | 3.38 |
| Diligence | 4.75 | 3.88 |

| Category | The Score (0 to 5) | Median Score (0 to 5) |
|---|---|---|
| Perfectionism | 3.00 | 3.63 |
| Prudence | 3.50 | 3.25 |
| **Openness to Experience** | 2.88 | 3.31 |
| Aesthetic Appreciation | 2.00 | 3.25 |
| Inquisitiveness | 2.75 | 3.13 |
| Creativity | 3.50 | 3.63 |
| Unconventionality | 3.25 | 3.38 |
| Altruism | 4.25 | 3.88 |

Jennifer Barcelos:

# NON-PROFIT WORLD TO CREATING HER OWN MONEY

"I was tired of having to ask for money in the nonprofit world." —Jennifer

Jennifer doesn't have to ask for money anymore. She makes it herself.

Jennifer was an environmental attorney from the San Juan Islands in Washington before she joined Start From Zero. Before, she spent her time asking rich people for money. Now that she has her own business, she spends her time working on what she loves, raising her daughter, and serving on the boards of nonprofits.

She wakes around 6:45 a.m. and works five hours a day. She's done by noon. Pretty sweet.

Jennifer transformed a series of beliefs to get where she is. Coming from the nonprofit world, she believed that money was hard to get, and now she believes money is just another form of energy. When I asked her about her greatest fear, she said, "My greatest fear was being embarrassed that entrepreneurship wasn't as 'meaningful' as the work I was doing before."

That would be a sneaky thought if you let it rule you, wouldn't it?

But her deeper "why" was beautiful: "I want to live a life on my own terms. That means time with my family, but also the financial freedom to go back to some of the service-based work I was doing before (without having to rely on a nonprofit salary to support me)."

When I asked her how many times she had thought of giving up... "Seriously? Never. Though I have cried about it a few times."

She used to believe that she didn't "get" tech. Now she believes she can do anything she wants to put the effort into learning. That's good considering she owns a SaaS business.

Before she believed she didn't have the training, so it would be hard. Now she believes it's an asset not to have the formal training. (I usually have to un-teach people what they've learned, by the way.)

And lastly, she thought luck was everything. Now she believes luck is involved, but it isn't everything.

You can see across each belief she transformed that she became more and more empowered. Remember, the foundation for freedom of thinking is boiled down to one question. Does this thought produce freedom? If you go through each one of Jennifer's beliefs, you see that the new belief creates more freedom.

Jennifer is a brilliant thinker. Her path to success was very fun to watch. Here's what happened.

She interviewed 74 yoga studios, asking them about their most painful problems, and created a 14-page document called "Software Challenges Yoga Studios Face" as part of her research. Every conversation she had created a little more information for her document. By putting this document together, she accidentally positioned herself as an expert in tech within the yoga industry and was invited to speak at events. She said, "Yes."

The report led her to create NamaStream.com—which I'll share more about shortly.

Let's break down Jennifer's business into customer, pain, solution, and offer.

**Who's your customer?**
Yoga teachers, yoga studios, gyms, female entrepreneurs, and health coaches.

**What's their pain?**
Wanting growth, but not having the risk that comes from expanding a brick-and-mortar operation.

**What's your solution?**
Namastream.com
Namastream allows wellness practitioners to teach online to anyone from anywhere. And now Jennifer has The Soulful MBA Info Product Course.

**What's your offer?**
NamaStream: $125 a month to $179 a month, depending on how many teachers you have.

The Soulful MBA Info Product Course: ~$1,800 for their training + a free Namastream subscription for a year.

## Jennifer's three tips:

1. It's a long game. Enjoy the process and allow yourself the grace to make mistakes and learn from them.

2. Treat every setback or instance of rejection as a learning opportunity. Have some goals and benchmarks, but never tie your worth and happiness to their achievement. You can't control everything. Base your happiness on stuff you can control (like your attitude).

3. People expect it to happen quickly and then give up once the newness starts to wear off. Enjoy day five hundred as much as day five.

# Jennifer Barcelos' Hexaco Score:

| Category | The Score (0 to 5) | Median Score (0 to 5) |
|---|---|---|
| Honesty-Humility | 3.38 | 3.22 |
| Sincerity | 4.25 | 3.25 |
| Fairness | 3.50 | 3.38 |
| Greed-Avoidance | 3.50 | 2.63 |
| Modesty | 2.25 | 3.63 |
| Emotionality | 3.63 | 3.34 |
| Fearfulness | 3.00 | 3.00 |
| Anxiety | 4.25 | 3.75 |
| Dependence | 3.75 | 3.25 |
| Sentimentality | 3.50 | 3.50 |
| eXtraversion | 3.06 | 3.50 |
| Social Self-Esteem | 3.50 | 4.00 |
| Social Boldness | 3.75 | 3.13 |
| Sociability | 2.25 | 3.63 |
| Liveliness | 2.75 | 3.63 |
| Agreeableness | 2.19 | 3.00 |
| Forgivingness | 1.50 | 2.75 |
| Gentleness | 1.75 | 3.25 |
| Flexibility | 2.75 | 2.75 |
| Patience | 2.75 | 3.25 |
| Conscientiousness | 3.63 | 3.47 |
| Organization | 3.75 | 3.38 |
| Diligence | 4.50 | 3.88 |
| Perfectionism | 3.25 | 3.63 |
| Prudence | 3.00 | 3.25 |
| Openness to Experience | 3.88 | 3.31 |
| Aesthetic Appreciation | 3.75 | 3.25 |

| Category | The Score (0 to 5) | Median Score (0 to 5) |
|---|---|---|
| Inquisitiveness | 3.75 | 3.13 |
| Creativity | 4.00 | 3.63 |
| Unconventionality | 4.00 | 3.38 |
| Altruism | 3.75 | 3.88 |

# EX-PEST CONTROL INSPECTOR BUYS HIS DREAM HOME

"I live in the types of homes I used to work for." —Mark

Mark gets to stay at home with his children all day and shoot bottles, dig potholes, and run on the open farmland in his dream home in Iowa. He never has to leave his kids to go to work.

*Ever.*

We were walking around his property when he pointed into the distance. "Dane, you see all this land over beyond the trees? I think I'm going to buy that, too, so no one can build a home around me." Wouldn't that be nice if we all had that kind of financial power?

Years ago, Mark was traveling around Des Moines as a pest control inspector, visiting the homes he wanted to live in. Envious. And confused. *How do you do it?* he thought. Then he heard about Start From Zero. Within four years of joining Start From Zero, he had left his job, built a million-dollar business, and grown his own SaaS company, as well.

He wakes up at 6:00 a.m. and works for five hours. By lunchtime, Mark is done with work. "I used to wake up, go to work all day, then come home exhausted, and do it all over again. Now I wake up feeling refreshed and love what I'm doing."

# How did Mark do it?

He transformed many crippling beliefs.

"In the past, I felt scarcity around money and thought money was limited. I believed that I really didn't have value to add to the world. I thought I was fat and out of shape. I was undisciplined."

"Now I realize that money is truly abundant, but you still have to put in the work. The only person who is going to hold me back from my goals is myself. I must look myself in the mirror every morning and decide to go to war with that person and do what I know I need to get done."

"Before I tried to work as many hours as I could to make enough to go on vacation. Now I've structured my life so I don't feel I need a vacation, and I just do what I want."

Mark created a Google Toolbar extension (HowManyExtension.com) that solves a very small problem for a niche market. He tried four different ideas before landing on this one.

It took Mark about six months for things to click. To learn his entrepreneurial skills, he started by finding a painful problem in the airline industry. He contacted an air flight controller, asked them about their painful problems, found a solution, sketched a solution out, got a verbal "yes" for a pre-sale, but then bad news struck. A big software company just released the product he was going to build, and he lost his customer. But with all those skills he had just learned, he started over and built what is now his successful software app.

His greatest fear was transitioning from employee to entrepreneur. *How am I going to do that?!* he thought. However, he has never thought of giving up. Being at home with his family was more important than his fear.

When you have the skills, you no longer have insecurity about losing a product idea. They become abundant. Let's break Mark's current success down into customer, pain, solution, offer.

**Who is your customer?**
People and businesses that sell on Amazon.

**What is their pain?**
Not knowing how much inventory their competitors have in stock. If competitors have a lot of inventory, it might be best to sell something else. This helps them.

**What's your solution?**
HowManyExtension.com
A Google Chrome extension that displays this information with little work so businesses can plan accordingly.

**What's your offer?**
$14.95 per month or $149.95 per year and access to the Chrome extension and mobile app.

# Mark's three tips:

1. Don't neglect marketing just because you don't like it. Find other people to do things for you that you don't like, but never neglect them. Continue improving yourself and learn new hobbies. Get 1% better every day. Remember yesterday was the easy day—now get after it!

2. Know your purpose. Why are you doing what you are doing? If you know that you won't give up. Next is certainty, trust in yourself and your abilities. Next, make sure you balance consumption and production. It is OK to consume and learn new things,but make sure you are also producing. If all you do is consume, you are just wasting time, and even though it feels good, you are producing nothing.

3. It's up to you. You have to decide. You must be the one who goes to war with yourself.

# Mark Crawford's Hexaco Scores:

| Category | The Score (0 to 5) | Median Score (0 to 5) |
|---|---|---|
| Honesty-Humility | 2.50 | 3.22 |
| Sincerity | 2.50 | 3.25 |
| Fairness | 2.75 | 3.38 |
| Greed-Avoidance | 2.00 | 2.63 |
| Modesty | 2.75 | 3.63 |
| Emotionality | 3.19 | 3.34 |
| Fearfulness | 2.50 | 3.00 |
| Anxiety | 4.00 | 3.75 |
| Dependence | 3.00 | 3.25 |
| Sentimentality | 3.25 | 3.50 |
| eXtraversion | 3.13 | 3.50 |
| Social Self-Esteem | 3.50 | 4.00 |
| Social Boldness | 3.50 | 3.13 |
| Sociability | 1.75 | 3.63 |
| Liveliness | 3.75 | 3.63 |
| Agreeableness | 3.13 | 3.00 |
| Forgivingness | 3.00 | 2.75 |
| Gentleness | 3.00 | 3.25 |
| Flexibility | 3.00 | 2.75 |
| Patience | 3.50 | 3.25 |
| Conscientiousness | 2.94 | 3.47 |
| Organization | 3.00 | 3.48 |
| Diligence | 2.75 | 3.88 |
| Perfectionism | 3.50 | 3.63 |
| Prudence | 2.50 | 3.25 |
| Openness to Experience | 2.81 | 3.31 |
| Aesthetic Appreciation | 2.50 | 3.25 |

| Category | The Score (0 to 5) | Median Score (0 to 5) |
|---|---|---|
| Inquisitiveness | 3.25 | 3.13 |
| Creativity | 3.25 | 3.63 |
| Unconventionality | 2.25 | 3.38 |
| Altruism | 4.50 | 3.88 |

# Amar Ghose:

# HE NO LONGER USES
# AN ALARM CLOCK

"I travel the world most of the year." —Amar

*Beep. Beep.*
*Beep.*
*Beep.*

The piercing sound of Amar's alarm clock is now a distant memory. So is his three-hour commute.

"Bye, Felicia!"

Amar is now free.

But Amar didn't have entrepreneurship in his life plan. He told me, "I would have probably worked a sales job for the rest of my life, or maybe done marketing for someone else, likely in San Francisco. Being indoors all the time, I'd slowly but surely turn into a vampire from the lack of sun."

Amar used to spend nine hours a day in the office plus three hours commuting by train. Yuck. That's a 12-hour workday. That's not a great way to spend your time.

Then he joined Start From Zero. And got his transformation.

Today he spends 10 months a year outside of the US and has a team of 15 people across the world. They meet in various spots like Morocco or Thailand.

Amar worked hard to get his business off the ground... At the start, he spent more than 12 hours a day for two years. Now he works four to six hours a day and takes time off whenever he wants. He spends his time working out, cooking, and taking naps when he wants to optimize his energy. He spends about three months in each place he travels to.

"I love it," he says.
Of course, he does. He's not answering to anyone anymore.

One very interesting thing I find exciting in many of these cases is their book choices before and after their transformations. In Amar's case, he used to read books like *The 4-Hour Workweek* and now reads books like *Principles* by Ray Dalio.

One book promises a result. The other is a commitment to a process. It's not wrong to like the former; it's just human nature. You want to get out of your painful situation, so you are drawn to books like *The 4-Hour Workweek*. Then as you transform and claim your best life, you start becoming concerned with deeper topics that focus on process. A book like *Principles* will start to resonate. This has been true in each student transformation I've encountered.

That's because the transformation is real. Your entire vibrational field changes, so you start to become interested in different things. It's really dang cool.

Amar thinks he was a slow bloomer. He said it took him four years before things really clicked and flowed for him (although he left his job much sooner than that). His company is now in its fifth year and doubled revenues last year!

To find ZenMaid, they entered a couple of other industries and then landed on maid service companies. Amar started contacting maid service companies and found out about a deep problem with scheduling and logistics for maid teams.

Amar told me, "My greatest fear when starting was missing other opportunities that could get me where I wanted to go faster—but that fear passed quickly."

"I've wanted to give up more times than I can count on one hand. My partner and I were close to throwing in the towel on multiple occasions, both together and individually. I think that changed after three to four years when we became a little more stable financially."

But his deeper "why" was clear, and it kept him moving through. "I've always been focused on the lifestyle afforded by time and location independence. ZenMaid started as a way to achieve that, but it's turned into much more. I now wake up more excited about my team and customers than my own life interests."

You can see Amar is evolving beyond himself. It's beautiful to witness.

Let's break Amar's business down into customer, pain, solution, and offer.

**Who's your customer?**
Maid services and housekeeping companies.

**What's their pain?**
Managing their calendars, reminders, and more is both time consuming and an easy place to make mistakes (when doing manually).

**What's your solution?**
ZenMaid.com
ZenMaid automates a variety of tasks and does quite a few things that a person can't (like reporting).

**What's your offer?**
$49 per month + $9 per month per employee for access to all features.

His rough revenue for the business is $500,000 ARR (annual recurring revenue).

## Amar's three tips:

1. Document what you are doing from day one to improve on then pass on everything that you did.

2. Focus heavily on marketing and sales, as you create the momentum for other things to build later (like a team).

3. Just get started; find an idea that's so good you can recruit a top developer to work on it with you without paying them.

## Amar Ghose's Hexaco Score:

| Category | The Score (0 to 5) | Median Score (0 to 5) |
|---|---|---|
| Honesty-Humility | 2.69 | 3.22 |
| Sincerity | 2.75 | 3.25 |
| Fairness | 1.75 | 3.38 |
| Greed-Avoidance | 2.50 | 2.63 |
| Modesty | 3.75 | 3.63 |
| Emotionality | 2.25 | 3.34 |
| Fearfulness | 2.50 | 3.00 |
| Anxiety | 2.00 | 3.75 |
| Dependence | 2.50 | 3.25 |
| Sentimentality | 2.00 | 3.50 |
| eXtraversion | 4.50 | 3.50 |
| Social Self-Esteem | 5.00 | 4.00 |
| Social Boldness | 4.50 | 3.13 |
| Sociability | 4.75 | 3.63 |
| Liveliness | 3.75 | 3.63 |
| Agreeableness | 3.13 | 3.00 |
| Forgivingness | 2.50 | 2.75 |
| Gentleness | 3.50 | 3.25 |

| Category | The Score (0 to 5) | Median Score (0 to 5) |
|---|---|---|
| Flexibility | 3.50 | 2.75 |
| Patience | 3.00 | 3.25 |
| **Conscientiousness** | 2.44 | 3.47 |
| Organization | 2.00 | 3.38 |
| Diligence | 3.00 | 3.88 |
| Perfectionism | 2.00 | 3.63 |
| Prudence | 2.75 | 3.25 |
| **Openness to Experience** | 3.06 | 3.31 |
| Aesthetic Appreciation | 2.25 | 3.25 |
| Inquisitiveness | 2.75 | 3.13 |
| Creativity | 3.75 | 3.63 |
| Unconventionality | 3.50 | 3.38 |
| Altruism | 3.50 | 3.88 |

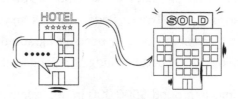

# FROM HOTEL TECH SUPPORT, TO SELLING THREE COMPANIES

"I used to believe you had to work in an office to have security. Now I know you do not. My "why" is my family and their well-being. Also, I want my two sons to see that their father doesn't give up on things, and eventually, I would like to have a business that they can take over should they want it."

— Geordie

Geordie is one of the most outgoing, upbeat dudes I have ever met. I love this guy's optimism. My messages from Geordie usually go something like... "Yo, Dane!!! Waoooooooo!!!!"

Geordie used to work as an Oracle database administrator in South America. Then he joined Start From Zero. He started doing idea extraction on hotels in South America and found a big pain with hotels getting bad online reviews—it would kill their bookings. He found a developer who partnered on the deal and built his first software business at no cost for sharing equity and built the business up to $10,000+ a month. That business is called WaveReview.com.

Then he started selling big bags of salt online. Then sold that business. And then he started another business. And then another...

The dude got creative.

Presently, he's working on developing a lead generation software product. He plans to use AI to sift through massive amounts of leads that people post on places like Instagram, Twitter, Reddit, forums, and websites. Based on the criteria he plans on building in, users will grade the leads so that the machine learning can get better at judging a good lead from a bad lead.

Currently, he brings in around $500,000 in net income. He's currently living in Bermuda (Bahama, come on, pretty mama!).

(What? Bad joke?)

(OK, OK...)

Now he only works on what interests him and moves on if he doesn't like it. He has full freedom of choice on his projects. He went from working nine hours a day to six to eight hours a day.

When I asked Geordie what his greatest fear was, he told me, "I don't really have fear at this point. I get frustrated, but I am not afraid. I am too determined to become afraid. Perhaps, I am afraid that my project will take too long to gain traction and that I will run out of money. So far, this hasn't happened, and if it does, I know that I will do whatever it takes to make money to keep the lights on and keep working on my projects."

For Geordie, it took him around six months to gain enough skills that he could start a business on his own. He's never thought of giving up, only changing projects. He's started five companies now and sold three of them and is especially passionate about his current project.

Let's break down Geordie's most recent business into customer, pain, solution, and offer.

**Who's your customer?**
Geordie: Customers in the $2 to $10 million revenue range that need marketing help with lead generation services.

**What's their pain?**

Geordie: They can't find enough software projects to keep their developers busy full-time. There are gaps where they find expensive developers sitting still. They need a constant supply of leads.

**What's your solution?**

I'm building AI to find suitable candidates (leads) from their ideal client avatar. Based on machine learning and custom attributes, software developers can now focus on development while their leads come in automatically.

**What's your offer?**

Geordie: $75 to $200 per month.

When I asked Geordie about entrepreneurship, here's what he had to say.

"Entrepreneurship is exactly what I was born to do. I can feel that in my deepest subconscious. Entrepreneurship to me is about much more than just money. Yes, the freedom is nice, but with freedom comes a lot of self-discipline and stress. There is no one else you can fall back on to ask for advice. When things are not working, you are alone. You are the only one that can fix your problems. You will get stuck, and there will be challenges. But this is the part that I love. The feeling of breaking through problems is so rewarding that it will keep you moving forward. At this point, I can't imagine any other life. To me, going back to an office is no longer an option. I would change my living situation to maintain entrepreneurship before doing that. The idea of finally achieving my real potential also keeps driving me forward with relentless determination."

# Geordies three tips:

1. Focus on having fun.
2. Find a good problem to solve.
3. If you don't like a project, don't be afraid to move on to another.

# Geordie Wardman's Hexaco Score:

| Category | The Score (0 to 5) | Median Score (0 to 5) |
|---|---|---|
| Honesty-Humility | 3.81 | 3.22 |
| Sincerity | 3.50 | 3.25 |
| Fairness | 5.00 | 3.38 |
| Greed-Avoidance | 3.25 | 2.63 |
| Modesty | 3.50 | 3.63 |
| Emotionality | 1.88 | 3.34 |
| Fearfulness | 1.00 | 3.00 |
| Anxiety | 1.50 | 3.75 |
| Dependence | 1.75 | 3.25 |
| Sentimentality | 3.25 | 3.50 |
| eXtraversion | 4.13 | 3.50 |
| Social Self-Esteem | 4.75 | 4.00 |
| Social Boldness | 3.75 | 3.13 |
| Sociability | 3.00 | 3.63 |
| Liveliness | 5.00 | 3.63 |
| Agreeableness | 4.13 | 3.00 |
| Forgivingness | 3.50 | 2.75 |
| Gentleness | 4.00 | 3.25 |
| Flexibility | 4.00 | 2.75 |
| Patience | 5.00 | 3.25 |
| Conscientiousness | 3.81 | 3.47 |
| Organization | 3.50 | 3.38 |
| Diligence | 5.00 | 3.88 |
| Perfectionism | 2.25 | 3.63 |
| Prudence | 4.50 | 3.25 |
| Openness to Experience | 3.94 | 3.31 |
| Aesthetic Appreciation | 2.75 | 3.25 |

| Category | The Score (0 to 5) | Median Score (0 to 5) |
|----------|--------------------|-----------------------|
| Inquisitiveness | 4.25 | 3.13 |
| Creativity | 4.50 | 3.63 |
| Unconventionality | 4.25 | 3.38 |
| Altruism | 5.00 | 3.88 |

# SHE WORKS ANYWHERE SHE WANTS

"I used to sell shoes, now I work from home." —Sandy

Sandy lives where it's cold, in Calgary, Alberta, Canada. She used to believe her identity was defined solely by her education and career. She had a fixed mindset around who she was...and was unsure about her own ability to start a new career and company. "I didn't believe there was much ability to change," she'd tell me.

Sandy used to sell shoes at her own store. Now she owns a SaaS business called Connectable.biz and has also partnered with Jennifer of Namastream.

"Today, my mornings are walking the dog and getting my son to school, then working on the businesses. Then in the late afternoon, I go for a workout, then have dinner and time with my family." She doesn't "have to show up" anywhere now.

Now she says, "My entire identity has shifted. I can do and have whatever I want. Truly...anything is mine for the taking. I learned that I was not simply a function of my education and past accomplishments but that I was a whole lot more complex than I initially knew! I learned I could gain new skills as I went along and that nothing at all was fixed. Every aspect of myself, both inner and outer, was in a state of growth, and I just needed to pay attention to those areas to see things flourish."

Here's how she found her idea...
"I followed the model in Start From Zero. I tossed around a few ideas before I realized that I was experiencing a pain every week at my networking group. I started phoning groups around North America and found that everyone was experiencing the same pain. Sharing leads amongst each other."

That's what area networking groups do—share leads and referrals.

Things started clicking for Sandy after a couple of years; however, she was one of the fastest to get her software made in around eight months.

She tried around three business ideas to land on her current one and has thought of giving up "maybe two times." But it's just not an option for her because, as she says, "What else would I do?"

Her deeper why is: "I want to be challenged and always learning. It's also important that I am creating something that makes people's lives better. But more than anything, I want to be in control of how I spend my days. I don't ever want someone dictating how I use my time."

Let's break down Sandy's business, Connectable.biz, into customer, pain, solution, and offer.

**Who's the customer?**
Professional networking groups.

**What's their pain?**
Networking groups were sharing leads on pieces of paper at their weekly meetings. Also, the administrator was typing up those leads and sending out newsletters. Everything was done manually in spreadsheets, word processor, and pen and paper.

**What's the solution?**
Connectable.biz
Connectable allows them to share leads throughout the week instead of at the meetings. It also automates newsletters and attendance and

makes all group communication more efficient and organized. It saves the members and administrators time.

**What's the offer?**

$7 per member per month.

And her rough income from this business is $60,000 to $80,000 a year.

## Sandy's three tips:

1. Don't be afraid to partner with a good developer who can handle all of the intimidating tech.

2. Be curious. You can do super hard things if you stay curious.

3. Be careful of expecting results too quickly and expecting others to solve your problems for you. It's all up to you, and you need to be in it for the long haul.

## Sandy Connery's Hexaco Score:

| Category | The Score (0 to 5) | Median Score (0 to 5) |
|---|---|---|
| **Honesty-Humility** | 3.75 | 3.22 |
| Sincerity | 3.50 | 3.25 |
| Fairness | 4.75 | 3.38 |
| Greed-Avoidance | 2.00 | 2.63 |
| Modesty | 4.75 | 3.63 |
| **Emotionality** | 3.31 | 3.34 |
| Fearfulness | 2.50 | 3.00 |
| Anxiety | 2.00 | 3.75 |
| Dependence | 4.25 | 3.25 |
| Sentimentality | 4.50 | 3.50 |
| **eXtraversion** | 4.75 | 3.50 |
| Social Self-Esteem | 4.75 | 4.00 |

| Category | The Score (0 to 5) | Median Score (0 to 5) |
|---|---|---|
| Social Boldness | 4.50 | 3.13 |
| Sociability | 5.00 | 3.63 |
| Liveliness | 4.75 | 3.63 |
| Agreeableness | 3.94 | 3.00 |
| Forgivingness | 3.75 | 2.75 |
| Gentleness | 4.25 | 3.25 |
| Flexibility | 3.50 | 2.75 |
| Patience | 4.25 | 3.25 |
| Conscientiousness | 3.31 | 3.47 |
| Organization | 4.00 | 3.38 |
| Diligence | 4.25 | 3.88 |
| Perfectionism | 3.00 | 3.63 |
| Prudence | 2.00 | 3.25 |
| Openness to Experience | 4.00 | 3.31 |
| Aesthetic Appreciation | 3.50 | 3.25 |
| Inquisitiveness | 5.00 | 3.13 |
| Creativity | 4.00 | 3.63 |
| Unconventionality | 3.50 | 3.38 |
| Altruism | 4.75 | 3.88 |

## Carl Mattiola:

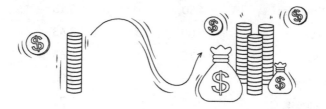

# SIX FIGURE EMPLOYEE TO MULTI-MULTI-MILLIONAIRE

"I was never happy working for someone else." —Carl

Carl owns his own full-on enterprise. He's the number one fastest-growing company in his industry, with 30 employees. He used to work at Tesla as an employee. Now...he works less than when he was at Tesla.

And makes a lot more money too.

Carl joined Start From Zero with a set of crippling beliefs. He struggled with self-expression and confidence for the first two years on his own path. He worked hard to change his beliefs. After six months, he was at $4,000 a month. Within three years, he got to $15,000 a month—and now, after six years, his business generates well over $5,000,000 a year, although he won't disclose how much more.

He "should" have been happy as a successful employee at Tesla. But he wasn't. His heart knew he was meant for more.

As I mentioned earlier in the book, Carl went through many transformations to get to where he is today. What I want to highlight with Carl is how remarkable he is at leadership. He's a role model for me and many others.

In less than five years, look at what Carl says today...

"I believe and know I can create an extraordinary life. I want to contribute to the world by helping over one billion people solve their pain naturally and fix the broken healthcare system, where addictive pain meds and dangerous surgery is recommended first for profit. People who try physical therapy and exercise first can have better outcomes and less expense. I want to work on that vision with an amazing team and to create a place to work where they get to live the lives they want to live and show up as themselves. I want to do all of this and have an amazing life of love and adventure with my wife, family, and friends."

What happened for Carl to get there? How did Carl start a business while working at Tesla? He woke up two hours earlier every day before Tesla and emailed and called Physical Therapy practices to find their biggest pain points.

Carl was relentless. He didn't even let his beliefs stop him. Carl is the kind of guy that takes action even if he is crippled. Because he was fighting his own belief systems, he was burning out and taking ice baths just to get to sleep. He didn't wait to be comfortable to take action.

Carl is not fearless, but he acts that way. His mind has learned to see that the area of his greatest fear is the best place he should go. Carl had many insecurities about his business and big fears. So what he did was face the greatest fears about his own business. And each time he did, his business would grow and innovate in a big way. So, he just started doing that more often.

But he has a different relationship with fear than most. He loves to surf. If there happens to be a great white shark attack at a location, he will go and surf there the next day because no one else will be there.

"Sharks don't really attack the same place twice," he told me. So, in a way, you'd say he's "fearless." But really, he's able to look fear straight in the eye with a smile and still take action. It's a powerful leadership quality. I'm very humbled by it.

Here's his business journey in his own words.

> "I interviewed hundreds of practice owners (via idea extraction). I then came up with several business ideas and started with ClinicMetrics because it was the easiest win. I knew that the issue of healthcare consolidation was the biggest problem in the market but wasn't sure how to tackle it. I met my now business partner during idea extraction, and we became friends over time. We partnered on a business using his systems and selling his procedures to other PTs. We tried selling newsletters as a solution. That failed. We then iterated to a course on marketing and lead generation for PTs, which took off. Then I used the money from that to fund the development of the idea for the platform, which is now the largest part of our business and key to realizing our purpose of helping people get back to normal naturally."

Chad famously rejected Carl when Carl first reached out. Chad sent Carl an email that said, "I don't have any problems, thanks for reaching out though." And instead of ignoring that reply, Carl said, "Hey, that's great, maybe you can tell me what's working well? I'm curious."

And through that, a friendship was formed.

It took Carl two years for his transformation to click and four ideas to land on his current platform. His greatest fear when starting was being an absolute failure, but he's never thought of giving up once. His deeper "why" keeps him going.

"For me, it's about leaving an impact on the world and helping to solve a problem for the greater good, as well as creating a place for others to work where they can live the lives they want to live...like I wanted when I was an employee." This drives Carl.

Let's break Carl's latest business product down into customer, pain, solution, and offer.

### Who's your customer?

We have two customers: physical therapy practices and people in pain with musculoskeletal issues (back pain, neck pain, shoulder pain, problems with balance and dizziness, arthritis, etc...)

### What's the pain?

For PTs: Healthcare is consolidating. PT practices usually get their referrals from physicians. Physicians are now being acquired by hospital systems and corporations and are forced to refer patients in house and often to surgery and pain meds first because of profit. Because of this, physician referrals to PT practices have dropped over 50% in the last eight years. PTs are losing their source of customers. We solve this problem through effective online marketing.

For Patients: They are getting addicted to pain medication and often getting surgery that is crazy expensive and does not always solve the real issue. People are left with their physical pain unsolved and often in a state of extreme frustration and helplessness. We show them how they can solve their pain naturally by connecting them to PT practices that can help.

### What's the solution?

ClinicMetrics.com

BreakthroughPTMarketing.com

We've built a platform guaranteed to send patients into PT practice from the general public (directly marketing to patients). When a practice signs up for our platform, we transform the health of their community by educating the public about how they can solve their musculoskeletal issues naturally, without pain meds or surgery. Through online advertising and automation, patients attend free workshops that the platform promotes, and we teach the practice how to convert attendees into patients. They regularly hear stories of surgeries being canceled and medication being stopped. From a business standpoint, they will often save a PT from going under and become their largest source of income overnight.

**What's the offer?**
PTs can be the only practice getting leads in each geographic area and also for each condition. Area exclusive marketing program by condition (back pain, shoulder pain, etc.).

## Carl's six tips:

1. Invest in yourself. "I'd double down on the amount I spent investing in programs to go even faster."

2. You must change your own beliefs. This is the most important thing I've learned in my life.

3. Learn about limiting beliefs and how to reverse them.

4. Know what you want. In life and in business. Write it down and look at it daily.

5. Understand a customer's biggest problem and then solve it.

6. Try stuff and fail, then try again. Failure is 100% necessary. Feel fear and act anyway. The number one thing that will get in your way is you. Reverse your limiting beliefs.

## Carl Mattiola's Hexaco Score:

| Category | The Score (0 to 5) | Median Score (0 to 5) |
|---|---|---|
| Honesty-Humility | 4.06 | 3.22 |
| Sincerity | 3.00 | 3.25 |
| Fairness | 5.00 | 3.38 |

| Category | The Score (0 to 5) | Median Score (0 to 5) |
|---|---|---|
| Greed-Avoidance | 4.25 | 2.63 |
| Modesty | 4.00 | 3.63 |
| **Emotionality** | 1.75 | 3.34 |
| Fearfulness | 1.50 | 3.00 |
| Anxiety | 1.25 | 3.75 |
| Dependence | 2.25 | 3.25 |
| Sentimentality | 2.00 | 3.50 |
| **eXtraversion** | 3.94 | 3.50 |
| Social Self-Esteem | 4.75 | 4.00 |
| Social Boldness | 4.00 | 3.13 |
| Sociability | 3.00 | 3.63 |
| Liveliness | 4.00 | 3.63 |
| **Agreeableness** | 3.69 | 3.00 |
| Forgivingness | 3.50 | 2.75 |
| Gentleness | 3.00 | 3.25 |
| Flexibility | 3.75 | 2.75 |
| Patience | 4.50 | 3.25 |
| **Conscientiousness** | 3.81 | 3.47 |
| Organization | 3.75 | 3.38 |
| Diligence | 5.00 | 3.88 |
| Perfectionism | 2.25 | 3.63 |
| Prudence | 4.25 | 3.25 |
| **Openness to Experience** | 3.50 | 3.31 |
| Aesthetic Appreciation | 2.50 | 3.25 |
| Inquisitiveness | 4.00 | 3.13 |
| Creativity | 3.50 | 3.63 |
| Unconventionallty | 4.00 | 3.38 |
| Altruism | 4.00 | 3.88 |

## Jeremy Chatelaine:

# SOFTWARE DEV BUILDS
# MILLION DOLLAR BUSINESS

"I didn't want to be a 60 year old software developer."–Jeremy

Jeremy is a father and husband from the UK. If you talk to him, you might think he's cynical, but he's just super real and damn inspiring if you listen. His alarm clock used to give him migraines. But he threw his alarm clock out and no longer has headaches. "I hated waking up at 7:00 a.m.," he told me.

But he works almost non-stop now. "I love it," he says.

Of course, who wouldn't love adding to their monthly revenue every single day? Jeremy's just playing at this point.

Jeremy had tried over 10 different business ideas on his own before joining Start From Zero...but he had a problem. He believed that selling was evil.

And now?
He thinks selling is noble. That it is a true gift: to offer a service to someone in need. When I asked him about his "why," and what kept him going, he said, "A developer is a shit job when you're old. I wanted long-term security."

Wait. Long-term security as an entrepreneur? You're damn right. When you do it correctly.

"Yesterday, I was snowboarding. Then I go to Bali for two weeks but to do deep work."

Jeremy is a no-fluff kind of guy. What you see is what you get. He's hungry. He's also a little stubborn. And it almost cost him this great idea. Thankfully he's smarter than he is stubborn :-).

Jeremy found his $70,000-per-month idea "by accident." While he was cold emailing businesses, he was getting tired of doing it manually. So, he built a little script for himself to automate the sending of emails.

Push a button, and it would send out a batch of emails. Come back the next day, push another button to see who did not reply. Then push another button to resend the email to anyone who had not replied, following up.

Students in Start From Zero got word of this script and started hounding him to get access to it, even sending him money to push him over the edge.

*I don't want to sell this product!* he thought. *I'm trying to find a problem with financial planners!*

What he didn't realize was that he had gold right under his nose, if he just looked down, and he was looking at a mountain of it. This is very common in business. The entrepreneur just resists what people want. Then ends up resenting the people, LOL. (I'm guilty too).

Let's break down Jeremy's business into customer, pain, solution, and offer.

### Who's your customer?
Lead generation agencies, small businesses, and individual entrepreneurs.

### What's their pain?
It's painful to keep track of all the outreach via cold email. However, I understand it's not really about my product; the deeper pain is that they need more leads.

**What's your solution?**
QuickMail.io
Automation of your own outbound email, including replies.

**What's your offer?**
It started at $9 a month, grew to $19, then to $29, and is now at $49 and $69 a month.
His rough revenue per month is over $70,000.

## Jeremy's three tips:

1. I wasted 10 years. Find an example of someone who did it and make it work. That was super inspirational. Flip business on its head; start selling before you build anything. And start by asking the right questions.

2. Be playful and try things. Most of the time, it works, which is strange. I have this ability to suspend belief and try it to see for myself. Don't build anything until it's sold.

3. I see the biggest thing stopping people is allowing distraction, lacking focus, and the inability to execute. Somehow people can't make it because they just won't level up. They do things to prevent the feeling of rejection. They get lost along the way. Some people are just in a loop, and you see them every year, and there is no progress. Stuck in the mud, speeding, and not moving.

## Jeremy Chatelaine's Hexaco Score:

| Category | The Score (0 to 5) | Median Score (0 to 5) |
|---|---|---|
| Honesty-Humility | 4.19 | 3.22 |
| Sincerity | 3.50 | 3.25 |
| Fairness | 4.25 | 3.38 |

| Category | The Score (0 to 5) | Median Score (0 to 5) |
|---|---|---|
| Greed-Avoidance | 4.50 | 2.63 |
| Modesty | 4.50 | 3.63 |
| Emotionality | 2.31 | 3.34 |
| Fearfulness | 2.75 | 3.00 |
| Anxiety | 2.00 | 3.75 |
| Dependence | 2.25 | 3.25 |
| Sentimentality | 2.25 | 3.50 |
| eXtraversion | 3.81 | 3.50 |
| Social Self-Esteem | 4.25 | 4.00 |
| Social Boldness | 3.50 | 3.13 |
| Sociability | 3.50 | 3.63 |
| Liveliness | 4.00 | 3.63 |
| Agreeableness | 3.19 | 3.00 |
| Forgivingness | 2.75 | 2.75 |
| Gentleness | 2.50 | 3.25 |
| Flexibility | 2.75 | 2.75 |
| Patience | 4.75 | 3.25 |
| Conscientiousness | 3.31 | 3.47 |
| Organization | 2.50 | 3.38 |
| Diligence | 5.00 | 3.88 |
| Perfectionism | 2.75 | 3.63 |
| Prudence | 3.00 | 3.25 |
| Openness to Experience | 3.06 | 3.31 |
| Aesthetic Appreciation | 2.00 | 3.25 |
| Inquisitiveness | 2.75 | 3.13 |
| Creativity | 3.50 | 3.63 |
| Unconventionality | 4.00 | 3.38 |
| Altruism | 4.25 | 3.88 |

Juliana Garcia:

# FROM CLIMBING THE LADDER, TO MAKING $60K IN A DAY

"I am easily the happiest and most fulfilled I've ever been." —Juliana

"When I was a little girl in Colombia, I thought that by moving to Australia, going to university and getting a high-paying job, I would be happy. My goal was to become a Marketing Executive in a Company and aim for a salary of around $200,000 per year. Later on, I realized that money wasn't the only thing that creates fulfillment—being aligned with your vocation is. The combination of both is where the sweet spot was for me."

Juliana used to wake up at 5:30 a.m. to hit her workout and get to work on time. It was very stressful. She spent her time in an office with people she didn't enjoy working with. She was stressed about her performance at work and what her boss was thinking of her. She felt that she was trying to comply with rules that she didn't agree with, just to keep people happy.

"Now I'm on my way to take my business to one million in 2019. I remember creating a vision board when I started Start From Zero, and now I see that I have created the life I once dreamed about. It took me five years, but I am now in a space where I'm allowing myself to create a vision beyond what I dreamed was possible."

Now she wakes up at a comfortable 7:30 a.m., hits the gym in her building, meditates, and journals every single morning before starting work. She still works seven hours a day but takes two to three months off every single year. So far, she's hit 49 countries and counting.

Now she works out of the comfort of her home office, with beautiful views of Chicago, creating content online that helps her connect with people all over the world. She's made many new like-minded friends and is leading women who want to create a business on their own terms.

She's got a structured schedule.
- Monday and Tuesday, she's working on her business without any distractions.
- Wednesday, she takes sales calls.
- Thursday and Friday, she serves her paying clients.

It took her about two years for things to click and flow, and she worked on three businesses before her current offer.

"I was really afraid of failing and looking bad in front of my friends. When I first started my current business with Soulful Marketing, and I started being active on social media spreading my message, I was afraid people would judge me for being 100% me."

Her "why" is: "My clients—just knowing that I helped one person reminds me there are many others."

Let's break down Juliana's business into customer, pain, solution, and offer.

### Who's your customer?
Female entrepreneurs (coaches and consultants) who are great at what they do, but marketing isn't their zone of genius. They need help communicating the value of what they do in a way that connects the hearts of their ideal clients and converts to sales.

### What's their pain?
They see old school marketing that uses guilt and shame and negative emotions to drive sales, and they don't know how to do it in a way that

feels good to them. They want to attract more clients but not at the cost of their own values. They want to attract clients with marketing that is profitable but also authentic to who they are. They compare themselves to more successful people and copy their message or business model, hoping it will bring them the same results. But it never does.

**What's your solution?**

JulianaGarcia.com

She's developed a signature method that helps clients:

1. Unlock their unique brilliance (define what makes them different from everyone else).
2. Create magnetic marketing that attracts their ideal clients.
3. Monetize their influence (after they grow their audience with the right people, the next step is to define a sales process that feels good to them so they can turn their audience into clients).

**What's your offer?**

1. Six months of 1:1 coaching (most popular).
2. Live group program "The exposed method."
3. VIP Days.
4. Self-paced program (eight-week course).

# Juliana's five tips:

1. If you have a dream or vision, don't wait for a miracle to happen to make it a reality. Start taking imperfect action today to get closer to that vision. Make it a daily habit to show up, give value, and make invitations for people to work with you.

2. Never doubt your value; you always have something valuable to share with the world. Start with what you know today.

3. (Mindset) Learn about how your brain works and how to rewire it so you can overcome old patterns and habits that you've picked up along the way.

4. (Marketing) Understand your ideal client better than they understand themselves. Get intimate with their world, empathize with them, and learn and how to communicate the value of what you do in a powerful way that connects with them.

5. The willingness to do uncomfortable things will take you far. Take the leap!

## Juliana Garcia's Hexaco Score:

| Category | The Score (0 to 5) | Median Score (0 to 5) |
|---|---|---|
| Honesty-Humility | 2.00 | 3.22 |
| Sincerity | 2.75 | 3.25 |
| Fairness | 1.75 | 3.38 |
| Greed-Avoidance | 1.25 | 2.63 |
| Modesty | 2.25 | 3.63 |
| Emotionality | 3.44 | 3.34 |
| Fearfulness | 3.00 | 3.00 |
| Anxiety | 4.50 | 3.75 |
| Dependence | 3.50 | 3.25 |
| Sentimentality | 2.75 | 3.50 |
| eXtraversion | 4.13 | 3.50 |
| Social Self-Esteem | 4.25 | 4.00 |
| Social Boldness | 4.25 | 3.13 |
| Sociability | 3.50 | 3.13 |
| Liveliness | 4.50 | 3.63 |
| Agreeableness | 2.69 | 3.00 |
| Forgivingness | 3.25 | 2.75 |
| Gentleness | 2.25 | 3.25 |
| Flexibility | 2.50 | 2.75 |

| Category | The Score (0 to 5) | Median Score (0 to 5) |
| --- | --- | --- |
| Patience | 2.75 | 3.25 |
| Conscientiousness | 3.31 | 3.47 |
| Organization | 2.25 | 3.38 |
| Diligence | 4.00 | 3.88 |
| Perfectionism | 3.75 | 3.63 |
| Prudence | 3.25 | 3.25 |
| Openness to Experience | 3.81 | 3.31 |
| Aesthetic Appreciation | 3.75 | 3.25 |
| Inquisitiveness | 4.00 | 3.13 |
| Creativity | 3.00 | 3.63 |
| Unconventionality | 4.50 | 3.38 |
| Altruism | 4.00 | 3.88 |

## Cris Urzua:

# HISPANIC EX-HOTEL EMPLOYEE CREATES A MILLION-DOLLAR BUSINESS

"Walk my dog, eat at home with my wife, do CrossFit, study for one hour, hit up work, eat some dinner with my wife—that's a good day for me."

—Cris

Cris lives in Cancun, Mexico. His success started fast, just three months after joining Start From Zero.

I still remember seeing Cris at the table, eating his lunch as a hotel employee. But that wasn't where Cris wanted to be. Cris had a goal for himself...to become a VP at a multinational hotel...earning a six-figure salary.

But instead, he made $1.2 million in his own business and now employs 30 people.

How did he get there?

He teaches the Hispanic market how to sell with heart by way of his business Selling Through Service. When he started, he didn't think that Latin American customers bought anything. He decided to put that belief to the test.

Cris's story is rather short because it all happened so fast once he got the skills he needed inside Start From Zero.

Cris studied business for four years before joining Start From Zero but still didn't know how to make it all work. Within three months, he had launched and made $10,000 in his first go. He tried three ideas before this: yoga retreats, restaurants, and a travel blog. He had big money fears when starting.

He had quit his job and had six months of basic living expenses saved. He spent half of it on Start From Zero and had to pay for a wedding six months later. But after his first launch, he never thought of giving up.

When I asked Cris about his "why," he said, "Creating a legacy I'm proud of, impacting people in a deep way, and seeing them change."

Let's break Cris's business down into customer, pain, solution, and offer.

**Who's your customer?**
Hispanic entrepreneurs and executives worldwide.

**What's their pain?**
Not enough sales. No confidence in their money-making skills.

**What's your solution?**
Urzua.mx
An online course called Selling Through Service—how to sell with heart.

**What's your offer?**
$997 for a three-month program.

## Cris's three tips:

1. Do it faster. Don't wait so long.

2. Focus on selling. 100%. Conversion is everything.

3. If you're being stopped, it is your mindset, 100%. Without a doubt. Get that fixed.

## Cris Urzua's Hexaco Score:

| Category | The Score (0 to 5) | Median Score (0 to 5) |
|---|---|---|
| **Honesty-Humility** | 3.13 | 3.22 |
| Sincerity | 3.25 | 3.25 |
| Fairness | 4.50 | 3.38 |
| Greed-Avoidance | 1.75 | 2.63 |
| Modesty | 3.00 | 3.63 |
| **Emotionality** | 3.25 | 3.34 |
| Fearfulness | 3.00 | 3.00 |
| Anxiety | 3.00 | 3.75 |
| Dependence | 3.50 | 3.25 |
| Sentimentality | 3.50 | 3.50 |
| **eXtraversion** | 3.75 | 3.50 |
| Social Self-Esteem | 4.25 | 4.00 |
| Social Boldness | 4.00 | 3.13 |
| Sociability | 3.25 | 3.63 |
| Liveliness | 3.50 | 3.63 |
| **Agreeableness** | 2.69 | 3.00 |
| Forgivingness | 3.25 | 2.75 |
| Gentleness | 2.75 | 3.25 |
| Flexibility | 2.25 | 2.75 |
| Patience | 2.50 | 3.25 |
| **Conscientiousness** | 3.94 | 3.47 |
| Organization | 4.25 | 3.38 |
| Diligence | 4.50 | 3.88 |
| Perfectionism | 3.00 | 3.63 |

| Category | The Score (0 to 5) | Median Score (0 to 5) |
|---|---|---|
| Prudence | 4.00 | 3.25 |
| **Openness to Experience** | 3.38 | 3.31 |
| Aesthetic Appreciation | 3.25 | 3.25 |
| Inquisitiveness | 3.50 | 3.13 |
| Creativity | 4.00 | 3.63 |
| Unconventionality | 2.75 | 3.38 |
| Altruism | 4.00 | 3.88 |

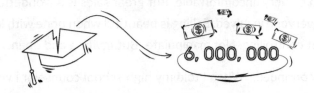

## Chandler Bolt:

# COLLEGE DROPOUT BUILDS SIX MILLION DOLLAR PER YEAR BUSINESS

"Make sure to do what you love."–Chandler Bolt

Chandler still drives his beat-up Nissan—but he's oceanfront living on prime Venice Beach real estate, at age 26.

"So,Chandler," I asked, "tell me about a few beliefs that you've transformed to become an entrepreneur."

He laughed. "I used to think it takes money to make money... Now, I know to sell first and build second."

We both laughed until our bellies hurt with that one. It's a pretty simple belief, but that one belief alone will free you.

"What other beliefs have you shifted?" I asked.

"Well I used to think you need a business plan or an LLC... Now, I know you just need sales to start a business. I also thought you needed a website and business cards to be in business... Now, I know you need sales and a product that solves a real problem."

There you go. Three variations of the same bellef. Things that are so obvious to us as entrepreneurs now, but at one time we never knew.

To the truly educated, selling is a noble act. To those with bad training, selling can be very uncomfortable. But great sales is a wonderful experience for everyone involved. Selling is beautiful when done with love. Not pushy. Not controlling. Not manipulate. But inviting and open.

Chandler continued, "When I told my high school counselor I wanted to be an entrepreneur, they suggested the next closest thing, which was to be a financial advisor," he told me.

"But, I shadowed one, and I was miserable. So, I didn't do that. And I figured, what the heck, I might as well go to college."

## The Day Chandler Decided to Leave for College

I'll never forget the day we were talking on the phone back when Chandler was in the midst of his transformation. He asked me...

"Dane, should I drop out of college?"

He was three months into Start From Zero at this point. My entire body screamed, "Yes!! Absolutely." But I asked him a few questions to help him come to his own conclusion. After he came to the same conclusion, I was relieved.

Dropping out of college is a serious life choice. You want to be sure a college degree supports your life vision. If you're going to be an engineer or a doctor, of course, stay. But for the land of entrepreneurship, get proper training with books, courses, and mentors, and get out there.

## Entrepreneurship vs. College.

Entrepreneurship is a naked feeling compared to college. Staying within the college system keeps you feeling that nice, safe, warm feeling. It's like a soft blanket. Entrepreneurship can feel cold at first until you realize there was never any blanket to begin with—just a highly competitive environment where college grads compete for the top jobs (usually) from businesses owned by C students or college dropouts.

There seems to be this associated risk with entrepreneurship versus college or being an employee. People often think:

College = comforting and safe.

Employee = someone takes care of you.

Entrepreneur = cold and uncertain.

That's how the uneducated mind can see it. But in fact, there is less risk in entrepreneurship when properly trained.

Yes. Less risk in entrepreneurship. You have more control over your income, multiple streams of income, and the chance to leave a large legacy of wealth for those you love.

As an employee you have one source of income, you do not really control your income, you depend on a company for it, and must save slowly over time to build a relatively small nest egg.

It's a very risky proposition to be an employee today, especially once your brain has been properly trained to be an entrepreneur. Just like Chandler and every other entrepreneur in this book who has been trained. You could take everything away from them, and they would build it all right back up.

So then where does the risk sit? Right in between your ears, inside your mind. And you have control over that.

Let's look at Chandler's business now...

**Who's the customer?**
Chandler has two customer avatars.

First, their largest customer is "Suzy," a 45 to 65-year-old female, impact-driven, recently an empty nester, has all this life experience, and wants to birth a second career to impact people, often faith-based, and sees a book as a way to help people.

Second, is "Jeff," who is 30 to 50, runs a business, and wants to write a book to grow leads for their business.

(Do you think there is a coincidence that he has a six-million dollar plus business and has these two customers so dialed in? I'll save you from guessing. It's not.)

**What's their pain?**
They are overwhelmed with the process of writing a book.

**What's your solution?**
Self-PublishingSchool.com
Go from blank page to published author in 90 days, with accountability.

They are an online education company that helps people write and sell books.
One-on-one coaching.
Weekly coaching.
Book editors.
Community.

**What's your offer?**
$3,000 to $5,000 depending on the package.

**Rough income or revenue?**
Six million per year.

## A Few of My Thoughts on Chandler

Chandler just works hard. I remember getting handwritten notes from the kid when he was 20. *Damn, this kid is going places*, I thought when I saw that card come in the mail.

Note that his income streams are very clearly broken into customer, pain, solution, and offer. As we know, these are the core components and building blocks that make up an income stream. It's great to look through that lens.

Second, notice how clear his offer is. Then, notice his revenue. Six million per year. That's an astounding feat for a college drop-out.

One million per year is around $2730 per day.

Six million per year is $16,500 or so per day.

If you look at his sale price of $3,000 to $5,000 per day, you see he needs to make only three to five sales a day to hit that. Doesn't seem so hard now, does it? There is nothing to hide from. Nothing to make excuses about anymore. No mystery. It's all here in this book.

You might find the skeptical part of you now saying... "Well, sure that's great, six million in revenue... How much does he keep?"

I'll just tell you it's way over one million dollars per year. Well over. And the kid is 26.

Have compassion for the skeptic inside. It's there for a reason. Do not override it. Welcome it in, and then ask if you can try another way. The skeptic has a few purposes. One is to keep you where you are. Don't let it do that to you.

Remember, compassion is often the missing ingredient to reach your goals faster. Compassion is the secret.

And all the details for how Chandler got his start are in this book. He was where you are now. He took the time to follow the process in this book.

## Chandler's Transformation Journey...

"One of my big early struggles as I was becoming successful was my conditioning around humility. I never wanted to make people feel like I was better than them because I know what it feels like."

Chandler had issues leading and managing people because he didn't want to seem better than them. After spending a ton of time on reflection, he saw his place as utilizing his God-given gifts and embraced them more. He spent a lot of time reflecting.

"I source my sense of self by maximizing the gifts and talents I've been given."

Chandler had two to three ideas before his big book business. He learned how to start a business while publishing his own books on the side for fun...and while his other businesses were struggling, people kept asking him how he was doing these successful books. So he'd tell them on the phone for free. Finally, he and his two friends turned it into a business and made $82,000 on their first launch.

It took Chandler two to three years for things to click and flow. He told me, "There's the iceberg, but then underneath is what actually happened. Always look for what's under the iceberg. Because we are not trained to see it."

His greatest fear when starting was that he'd fail after dropping out of school. And people would come out of the woodwork and tell him, "Hah, you were wrong!"

He almost took a job at one point when his cash was running out. But he stuck with it. His deeper "why" is big. He has two or three.

First, his friend passed away at 20 years old right in front of him. He felt like it was his fault. "The father told me that the only way this can be good is if good can come from this. So, I've been living for him since."

"I feel like I've been given God-given talents to run businesses, so I want to say, 'Hey, I left it all out on the table and the field.'"

He wants to retire his parents and make sure his family never has to worry about money.

## Chandler's three tips:

1. "Revenue is vanity, profit is sanity, and cash is king" is a quote by Keith Cunningham.

2. Use an extreme focus on getting the first customer and validation of ideas.

3. Fail as often and as fast as possible. Don't let anybody tell you that you shouldn't be failing. It's one of our core values at Self-Publishing School. The only way that you learn is to fail.

Before I got off the phone with Chandler, he kindly told me, "I would not have started this business had it not been for Start From Zero. Thank you, Dane."

## Chandler Bolt's Hexaco Score:

| Category | The Score (0 to 5) | Median Score (0 to 5) |
|---|---|---|
| Honesty-Humility | 3.13 | 3.22 |
| Sincerity | 3.00 | 3.25 |
| Fairness | 4.00 | 3.38 |
| Greed-Avoidance | 2.50 | 2.63 |
| Modesty | 3.00 | 3.63 |
| Emotionality | 2.25 | 3.34 |
| Fearfulness | 1.25 | 3.00 |
| Anxiety | 2.25 | 3.75 |
| Dependence | 2.75 | 3.25 |
| Sentimentality | 2.75 | 3.50 |
| eXtraversion | 4.38 | 3.50 |

| Category | The Score (0 to 5) | Median Score (0 to 5) |
|---|---|---|
| Social Self-Esteem | 4.75 | 4.00 |
| Social Boldness | 4.50 | 3.13 |
| Sociability | 3.25 | 3.63 |
| Liveliness | 5.00 | 3.63 |
| Agreeableness | 2.06 | 3.00 |
| Forgivingness | 2.00 | 2.75 |
| Gentleness | 1.50 | 3.25 |
| Flexibility | 2.25 | 2.75 |
| Patience | 2.50 | 3.25 |
| Conscientiousness | 4.06 | 3.47 |
| Organization | 4.25 | 3.38 |
| Diligence | 5.00 | 3.88 |
| Perfectionism | 3.00 | 3.63 |
| Prudence | 4.00 | 3.25 |
| Openness to Experience | 3.25 | 3.31 |
| Aesthetic Appreciation | 2.25 | 3.25 |
| Inquisitiveness | 3.25 | 3.13 |
| Creativity | 3.00 | 3.63 |
| Unconventionality | 4.50 | 3.38 |
| Altruism | 4.00 | 3.88 |

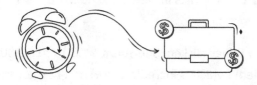

# SHE NOW OWNS A SAAS

"I believed that I could never succeed because I didn't have any value or worth. Now I have the belief that if you give me enough time, faith, and help, I can achieve anything I set my mind to."  — Maxie

Maxie is a young entrepreneur from New Zealand. She took our programs at the age of 22, and today she has enough income to be independent and work and live with one of her best friends.

She tells it straight: "I hated who I was, and I felt I had very little value or worth. I was angry at myself and my life. I felt a lot of shame and was embarrassed about what I had accomplished or failed to accomplish."

Maxie had planned to be a doctor who would work long hours and then use her high salary to invest in real estate. Like many in society, she believed that was the only way to get rich. "Now, I see that is not true."

Because then she got bit by the entrepreneurial bug. And it was a strong bite. She has never looked back and has not thought of giving up since. It took her two years for things to click and flow.

I keep telling you how much time it takes for things to click and flow because so many people give up before it works.

Maxie tried idea extraction on multiple niches. Property investors, real estate agents, acupuncturists in New Zealand...and then community acupuncturists in America.

And that's when things clicked. She spent $1,000 to $2,000 on her software development (which is incredibly low) and has generated $51,000 with her software to date. She sells many lifetime packages.

She's putting the nuts and bolts in place, and she has plans for seven-figure growth soon. But I wanted to include Maxie's story here because it was such a powerful transformation.

"My life plan now is to grow this business to make seven to eight figures within the next one to two years. Become a successful, financially free entrepreneur who can pursue being a professional artist—singing, performing, and acting. And then go on to build multiple companies—including social enterprises."

Maxie didn't start off with a vision like this. It's been six years since she started with Start From Zero, and she's been taking the time to reprogram her mind.

Maxie's product solves a very real problem for a group of now very happy people. Her current headline says, "Take Back 750 Hours Of Your Life Every Year." That's a dope headline for a now-confident entrepreneur. Check out her product at HappyCharting.com—the copy on this website is really solid.

One of her customers says, "I have been with Happy Charting from the beginning, and it has really changed the way I practice for the better."

Look at the impact she has now. From believing she had no value to receiving compliments like this. To really impacting the world. This could be you.

People seem to think things happen fast, but Colonel Sanders was 62 when he started KFC, and he had many failures before that. Take as long as you need on your journey. Please don't give up.

Let's look at Maxie's customer, pain, solution, and offer.

**Who's your customer?**
Acupuncture clinics in the USA and Canada, but she will eventually expand worldwide and to other niches.

**What's their pain?**
Charting is a pain to do. It's a daily repetitive task that takes time out of their day. To them, it feels like a chore that needs to be done for legal purposes. They *hate* charting.

**What's your solution?**
HappyCharting.com
Intuitive software they can personalize to suit their charting needs. Electronic Medical Records SaaS.

**What's your offer?**
Charting at $50/month.
All-in-One at $99 a month.

## Maxie's three tips:

1. Read *The Compound Effect*.
2. Join a course that teaches you what you need to learn, like Start From Zero.
3. Be mentored and learn from someone who's achieved what you want to achieve.

## Maxie Ouyang's Hexaco Score:

| Category | The Score (0 to 5) | Median Score (0 to 5) |
|---|---|---|
| Honesty-Humility | 3.69 | 3.22 |
| Sincerity | 3.75 | 3.25 |
| Fairness | 5.00 | 3.38 |

| Category | The Score (0 to 5) | Median Score (0 to 5) |
|---|---|---|
| Greed-Avoidance | 2.25 | 2.63 |
| Modesty | 3.75 | 3.63 |
| Emotionality | 3.25 | 3.34 |
| Fearfulness | 3.25 | 3.00 |
| Anxiety | 3.25 | 3.75 |
| Dependence | 3.00 | 3.25 |
| Sentimentality | 3.50 | 3.50 |
| eXtraversion | 4.19 | 3.50 |
| Social Self-Esteem | 4.75 | 4.00 |
| Social Boldness | 4.00 | 3.13 |
| Sociability | 4.00 | 3.63 |
| Liveliness | 4.00 | 3.63 |
| Agreeableness | 3.75 | 3.00 |
| Forgivingness | 4.50 | 2.75 |
| Gentleness | 3.75 | 3.25 |
| Flexibility | 2.75 | 2.75 |
| Patience | 4.00 | 3.25 |
| Conscientiousness | 2.69 | 3.47 |
| Organization | 2.75 | 3.38 |
| Diligence | 3.50 | 3.80 |
| Perfectionism | 2.75 | 3.63 |
| Prudence | 1.75 | 3.25 |
| Openness to Experience | 3.06 | 3.31 |
| Aesthetic Appreciation | 2.25 | 3.25 |
| Inquisitiveness | 3.00 | 3.13 |
| Creativity | 4.00 | 3.63 |
| Unconventionality | 3.00 | 3.38 |
| Altruism | 4.50 | 3.88 |

## Mr. Julian:

# LIVING HIS DREAM LIFE
# FROM THE UKRAINE

"Making a passive $20,000 per month business at home was so much easier than going to an office as a developer."    — Julian

Julian wanted to be anonymous, so he did not want his URL or last name mentioned here. He is one of those students I had who never joined my programs. He just listened to the free content I released. He is an excellent example because his Hexaco is an exception to our data.

"I used your free content on idea extraction to find my problem Dane," he told me.

Julian is awesome because he simply created a business around his Hexaco traits instead of fighting them.

"Instead of pushing through a lot, I just found my way around it," he said. "Because now I don't have to deal with social anxieties and other things that came up while working in an office full of people. I don't feel like I'm struggling at business because of some personality traits... I feel more like I found my own weird way of doing it and got good at it."

He gets drained talking to people all day, so he doesn't. He doesn't like having dozens of calls with customers and teams every day. So he doesn't do it. He built systems that support automated sales and hired a support engineer that does all of the communication with customers.

He runs his business in a low-risk way. He keeps his overhead small. Saves most of his income. And he's a lot less anxious since doing that.

As an entrepreneur, you get to be yourself. Not someone else.

Let's look at his customer, pain, solution, and offer.

**Who's the customer?**
Businesses with bigger marketing budgets in the $50,000+ range. His customers have 20 to 50 employees on average.

**What's the pain?**
Faulty sales attribution tracking. They don't know what's making them money and what is. Specifically they are not being able to track the source of the most profitable lead from inside their CRM platform. So they don't know if they are wasting money and time on poor leads.

**What's the solution?**
An integrated solution that shows which campaigns are profitable from inside the customer relationship management software like Salesforce. So they know which campaigns to keep investing in, and which campaigns to drop.

**What's the offer?**
$97 to $297 per month, depending on tiers.

## Julian's three tips:

1. Sell your solution as a service first. Validate it. Make some money, and then only turn it into an actual product.

2. Don't look at clicks or leads, always aim to measure the ROI of all your marketing activities. The discrepancy between top level metrics like clicks and the bottom line may surprise you.

3. Read the book "E-Myth." Automate what you can, and for what can't be automated, the solution is creating systems that allow you to have a business instead of a job.

## Jualian's Hexaco Score:

| Category | The Score (0 to 5) | Median Score (0 to 5) |
|---|---|---|
| Honesty-Humility | 2.81 | 3.22 |
| Sincerity | 4.00 | 3.25 |
| Fairness | 3.75 | 3.38 |
| Greed-Avoidance | 1.50 | 2.63 |
| Modesty | 2.00 | 3.63 |
| Emotionality | 3.88 | 3.34 |
| Fearfulness | 3.75 | 3.00 |
| Anxiety | 4.50 | 3.75 |
| Dependence | 4.00 | 3.25 |
| Sentimentality | 3.25 | 3.50 |
| eXtraversion | 2.63 | 3.50 |
| Social Self-Esteem | 3.00 | 4.00 |
| Social Boldness | 2.75 | 3.13 |
| Sociability | 2.25 | 3.63 |
| Liveliness | 2.50 | 3.63 |
| Agreeableness | 1.63 | 3.00 |
| Forgivingness | 1.25 | 2.75 |
| Gentleness | 2.00 | 3.25 |
| Flexibility | 1.75 | 2.75 |

| Category | The Score (0 to 5) | Median Score (0 to 5) |
|---|---|---|
| Patience | 1.50 | 3.25 |
| **Conscientiousness** | 3.00 | 3.47 |
| Organization | 2.50 | 3.38 |
| Diligence | 4.25 | 3.88 |
| Perfectionism | 3.00 | 3.63 |
| Prudence | 2.25 | 3.25 |
| **Openness to Experience** | 3.69 | 3.31 |
| Aesthetic Appreciation | 2.25 | 3.25 |
| Inquisitiveness | 3.75 | 3.13 |
| Creativity | 4.50 | 3.63 |
| Unconventionality | 4.25 | 3.38 |
| Altruism | 3.50 | 3.88 |

# The End.

## You officially know how to *Start From Zero*.

By the time you finish this book, you will see that you don't have to accept your present circumstance. You can create whatever it is you want with the proper training.

You can start from zero.

- May you see the brightest potential of your beautiful heart.
- May you find your voice in the business world.
- May you rock and roll with what you do.

I hope you enjoyed reading this book as much as I did creating it.

I'm not much for goodbyes.

So come and say hi to me at StartFromZero.com/Yes.

Signed,
--
Dane Maxwell

PS - What will you do now? Send me any and all results you get! As an author you'd be shocked at how many people never reach out to say thank you or hey. Don't worry. I won't bite. I'm only human. I look forward to hearing from you.

Just in case you missed it the first time...

Meet other people reading this book

*join the community at:*
StartFromZero.com/Yes

# THE BONUS ADVENTURES

The best books, blogs, resources, and courses you can read or buy.

Get every free BONUS PDF, checklist, worksheet, audio, interview, my bonus chapters, and more at StartFromZero.com/Yes.

You can find links to everything at StartFromZero.com/Yes

## Here are the top seven books I've read that changed my life (in order).

1.  *Rich Dad Poor Dad by* Robert Kiyosaki
    I had a romance with this book for the first 50 pages while still in the book store. I was riveted. I read it in two days. It gave me my entire spark for entrepreneurship.

2.  The *Law Of Success* by Napoleon Hill
    One thousand pages long, this took me three months to read, but I read every single page. When I finished reading this book, it was one of the greatest accomplishments of my life to date. My mother even saw the change in my heart from reading this book.

3.  *The Ultimate Sales Machine* by Chet Holmes
    I tripled my income by learning about Education Based Marketing, which is covered in this book. Gotta love some good ol' Chet.

4. *Power vs. Force* by Dr. David Hawkins

   This book gave me the feeling of grace and humility while still holding to my desire for accomplishment.

5. *Breakthrough Advertising* by Eugene Schwartz

   This gave me rock-solid confidence in marketing so I could execute with ease instead of being stuck in survival mode. This book helps with flawless marketing implementation. The seven distinctions for breakthrough copy are game changers.

6. *Stealth Marketing* PDF by Jay Abraham

   In the back of this book are three recorded transcripts of Jay's $5,000 coaching calls. You can see what he said to the people who paid him $5,000 for the hour. The best part is that each of these transcripts contains the same process from the first part of the book. So you read the principles then hear him implement the ideas into different business niches. And these people paid $5,000 to hear what you get to read. Technically a $15,000 value just in the transcripts.

7. *The Automatic Customer* by John Warrilow

   This book just makes you a wealthy person. The stats inside it are insane. You can read it in a couple days and transform your understanding of customer acquisition forever.

## Other Resources

Here is my favorite copywriting resource:

- Swiped.co/StartFromZero

Other great, free resources:

- My copywriting checklist, idea extraction guides, interviews with students, and more at: StartFromZero.com/Yes

The personality assessment:

* Hexaco.org – take the free personality assessment and then compare your answers to those from chapter one to see where you rank.

## Start From Zero Has Three Premium-Level Courses

MINDSET Help for Entrepreneurs:
6 Weeks To Becoming Friends With Your Own Mind

*For Beginners*:
The START Program: Learn How to Start a $20,000-Per-Month Business From Home Fast

*For Advanced*:
The ASSET Program: Learn How to Quickly Build Your Own Cash-Producing Assets From Scratch (Fifteen millionaire graduates and counting!).

Visit StartFromZero.com/Yes for more information on these courses.